Y0-BED-337

THE QUEST FOR CHURCH UNITY

THE MACMILLAN COMPANY
NEW YORK • CHICAGO
DALLAS • ATLANTA • SAN FRANCISCO
LONDON • MANILA

IN CANADA
BRETT-MACMILLAN LTD.
GALT, ONTARIO

THE QUEST FOR CHURCH UNITY

Matthew Spinka

New York
THE MACMILLAN COMPANY
1960

First Printing

The Macmillan Company, New York
Brett-Macmillan Ltd., Galt, Ontario

Printed in the United States of America

Library of Congress catalog card number: 60-5287

PREFACE

The substance of this book was originally delivered as Carew Lectures for 1958 at the Hartford Seminary Foundation, Hartford, Connecticut. The text of the fourth chapter was substantially rearranged, but the conclusions remained unchanged.

Why another book on Church unity? The principal reason is that my treatment constitutes an independent appraisal of the official proposals: since these latter are the result of many minds modifying one another, they thus represent the lowest common denominator or an irreducible minimum or maximum of consensus. Committees cannot work otherwise, particularly when they act in behalf of many conflicting Christian traditions. Accordingly, whatever merit this work possesses is owing to the fact that it offers the opinions of one earnestly concerned individual uninhibited by any official or group considerations. Needless to say, the responsibility for the expression of such convictions is entirely my own.

MATTHEW SPINKA

Claremont, California

CONTENTS

CHAPTER I

THE WORLD COUNCIL OF CHURCHES AND THE UNA SANCTA

The assumption has come to pass, I know not how, that the Great Church, or united Christendom, is at last within sight of becoming a reality. Church unity has been the fashion or passion of our age. The disunions and schisms of the past are roundly denounced as a scandal and a sin. Discussions about the "reunion" are sometimes carried on with more enthusiasm than insight, with more heat than light, although the shape of things to come is at present necessarily nebulous—a condition which leaves plenty of room for honest disagreement. In such circumstances the language used is often more vigorous than justified: to call loyalty to truth as others see it simply and unconditionally a sin is not only morally irresponsible but is itself a manifestation of that *odium theologicum* against which the ecumenicists themselves loudly protest. Honest conviction—even if regarded by some as erroneous—cannot be dealt with so cavalierly. To surrender present convictions for some vague future ideal in the belief that it would serve *ad majorem Dei gloriam* is a mistaken notion of the divine imperative. It is not an honest difference of opinion in religious matters which is sin; real sectarianism consists in complacency about the disunion and an intransigent attitude aiming to impose one's own convictions upon the Church as a whole. Some of the largest segments of Christendom are guilty of it.

But, on the other hand, since Christendom has never, throughout its twenty centuries, been actually and completely unified in the institutional or organic sense, should that unprecedented event ever take place, it would indeed be the greatest single step forward in its history. Accordingly, there is no topic which deserves and demands our sympathetic and prayerful attention more than this one. The Spirit of God, which is undoubtedly discernible in this movement, must not be quenched or ignored, although human motives mixed with it must be sternly discerned and subordinated to His will. I intend, therefore, to consider this supremely important subject sympathetically, fairly, and without prejudice; but likewise soberly, reasonably, critically, and with a clear awareness of its highly valuable as well as its illusory implications. The quest for unity must be conducted in truth and love. It would not help its cause to carry on a polite conversation that carefully avoids whatever might give offense to the other party, or to assume the uncritical attitude of a "mutual admiration society." Religious freedoms we have gained since the Reformation are too precious to be surrendered lightly.

In the first place, it is well to remind ourselves that although the modern ecumenical movement in its present form is less than a century old, it originated at least three centuries ago. In the seventeenth century—the era of tremendous ecclesiastical strife—three prominent figures represented the ecumenical pioneering efforts: John Dury, Georg Calixtus, and John Amos Comenius. My interest in this matter has been very considerable ever since my student years; in fact, I might confess that I had then been a somewhat uncritical enthusiast for Church unity. As a doctoral candidate at the University of Chicago I wrote my thesis on the subject of the ecumenical ideals and work of John Amos Comenius, and later wrote a book and articles dealing with this pioneer of ecumenicity. I have no reason to believe that my literary efforts have had the slightest influence or effect upon the ecumenical movement. But at any rate they show that from my earliest beginnings to the present I have given more than lip service to the cause. My interest and active efforts in promoting the study of Eastern Orthodox Christianity bear additional witness to my devotion to the cause. For many years I have specialized in such studies, for I was convinced that no ecumenical movement could be seriously undertaken without knowledge of Eastern Orthodoxy. I still hold the view, although I doubt that it has been seriously enough shared by others.

But passing over the remote origins of the movement—for such historical survey I refer the reader to *A History of the Ecumenical Movement* edited by Ruth Rouse and Bishop Stephen C. Neill, or an earlier work, *Unitive Protestantism* (1930), by John T. McNeill—let us turn our attention to the more recent beginnings of ecumenism which are to be found in the Chicago-Lambeth Quadrilateral of 1886–1888. In the earlier year, the General Convention of the Protestant Episcopal Church in the United States held its meeting in Chicago and adopted a four-point resolution aiming at restoring "the Christian unity now so earnestly desired. . . ." It consisted of four principles regarded as an irreducible minimum of such "reunion": (1) "The Holy Scriptures of the Old and New Testaments as the revealed Word of God; (2) The Nicene Creed as the sufficient statement of the Christian Faith; (3) The two Sacraments—Baptism and the Supper of the Lord—ministered with unfailing use of Christ's words of institution; (4) The Historic Episcopate, locally adapted in the method of its administration to the varying needs of the nations and peoples called of God into the unity of His Church." [1]

Two years later this proposal was adopted, with slight modifications, by the Lambeth Conference Committee on Home Reunion and has served henceforth as the basis of ecumenical proposals generally. The only important change affected the second article, where the Apostles' Creed was added "as the Baptismal Symbol" to the Nicene.

[1] From *A History of the Ecumenical Movement, 1517–1948,* edited by Ruth Rouse and Stephen Charles Neill (Philadelphia, The Westminster Press, 1954). Used by permission.

Nevertheless, although the desire for unity has penetrated to varying degrees most of the major Protestant communions, nothing of a decisive and practical character had occurred to implement it until 1910 when the World Missionary Conference was convened in Edinburgh. It was motivated principally by the need for cooperation on the mission fields, where the diversity of missionary societies, working often at cross-purposes, made the problem particularly painful. Some twelve hundred delegates attended. Doctrinal considerations, however, were ruled out. The two principal leaders of the conference were John R. Mott and J. H. Oldham; a young usher at the conference, named William Temple, then an Oxford tutor, and a personal friend of Mott, and later the Swedish archbishop Nathan Söderblom subsequently joined the older leaders as members of the team prominent in the ecumenical movement. As the result of the deliberations of the conference, the International Missionary Council was organized and has since played an important role in furthering the ecumenical aspirations. The resulting scheme aimed at missionary cooperation and comity, but in no sense essayed to break down the denominational barriers.

The demand for Church unity at home continued, and was effectively aided by other contributory causes: the two world wars, the "shrinking" of the world, the spread of secularism, the communist challenge to religion, and above all the growth of ecumenical consciousness. The threatening international situation which in the end broke out in the First World War aroused concern for world peace which served as an incentive for uniting Christendom. This effort received a mighty impetus from Andrew Carnegie who in 1913 provided funds for the establishment of the Church Peace Union. A grant from that organization made possible the holding of the first international conference at Constance, Germany. The delegates met on the very day that the war was declared—August 1, 1914. Under the circumstances the conference restricted itself to the election of international and national committees. The delegates then transferred their meeting to London, where they organized what was later known as the World Alliance for Promoting International Friendship through the Churches.

After the First World War, the Swedish archbishop Nathan Söderblom became the moving spirit of the ecumenical movement. Of tireless energy, he carried on tremendous correspondence with leaders of various churches. Despite the discouraging situation prevailing among the ecclesiastical communions of the former foe nations, the Scandinavian bishops persisted in their efforts to convene an international gathering as soon as possible after the war. In this effort Söderblom was not so successful as the International Committee of the World Alliance, which actually held a meeting in October, 1919, at Oud Wassenaar, Holland. There the German delegates, led by Adolf Deissmann, made a personal confession acknowledging the German war guilt and thus paved the way for the restoration of fraternal relations with the representatives of the Allied countries. The next year Archbishop Söderblom was able to convene a preliminary meeting in Geneva, but this accomplished very little of worth. Nevertheless, it succeeded in preparing the way for the Universal Conference on Life and Work, which met in Stockholm five years later. Some of the heartening events were the publication (1920) of the Lambeth Appeal to all Christian People and an Encyclical Letter by the Ecumenical Patriarch of Constantinople calling for cooperation between the Orthodox and Protestant churches.[2] This latter was particularly significant, because hitherto it had been thought well-nigh impossible to draw the Orthodox into such ecumenical discussions. The Stockholm Conference, "undoubtedly a landmark in the history of Christian churches since the Reformation," [3] was attended by 610 delegates representing 31 communions and 37 countries. Germans formed themselves into an isolated group. Among the leaders of the conference were William Adams Brown (American Presbyterian), A. E. Garvie

[2] L. A. Zander, *Vision and Action, the Problems of Ecumenism* (London, Victor Gollancz, Ltd., 1952), p. 98. Used by permission.

[3] Reproduced from *The Kingship of Christ* by G. K. A. Bell (Baltimore, Md., Penguin Books Inc., 1954).

(British Congregational), W. Monod (French Reformed), Siegmund-Schultze (German Lutheran), and Bishop G. K. A. Bell (Anglican), not to speak, of course, of Archbishop Söderblom, the prime mover of the conference. The underlying purpose was not so much a dogmatic discussion—in fact that was rigorously excluded on the ground that "doctrine divides, service unites"—as cooperation in the solving of practical problems confronting the post-war world as well as the churches. After a vigorous discussion, in which it became clear that even practical action rests ultimately on Christian convictions of varying kind, a message was adopted setting forth the findings of the conference in the spheres of economic, social, international, and interracial relationships. There were only four dissenting votes, based on the objection that the resolutions on the peace question did not go far enough. The Committee on Cooperation favored federation rather than organic union of the churches. Moreover, a Continuation Committee was appointed to prepare for greater things to come; interestingly enough, it appointed, among others, a theological commission, for it became clear that social action depended upon creedal and polity considerations.

Independently of this movement, other reunion efforts—mostly privately conducted, not involving corporate bodies officially—were carried on: thus between 1921 and 1925 the so-called Conversations of Malines in Belgium were conducted between the Anglicans, represented by Lord Halifax along with some eminent Anglican scholars, and the Roman Catholics, headed by Cardinal Mercier. Since Pope Leo XIII had declared, as early as 1896, the Anglican orders absolutely null and void, the conversations could not possibly result in anything but frustration. Monsignor Batiffol regarded any idea of reconciliation as utopian. Nevertheless, he thought that the conversations might perhaps encourage the Anglo-Catholics "in a Catholic direction." [4] In 1928 Pope Pius XI, without explicitly naming the ecumenical movement, declared in his encyclical *Mortalium animos:* "There is but one way in which the unity of Christians may be fostered, and that is by furthering the return to

[4] Rouse and Neill, *op. cit.,* p. 299.

the one true Church of Christ of those who are separated from it; . . . The one Church of Christ is visible to all, and will remain, according to the will of its Author, exactly the same as he instituted it. . . . Furthermore, in this one Church of Christ no man can be or remain who does not accept, recognize, and obey the authority and supremacy of Peter and his legitimate successors." [5]

The Anglicans in the meantime carried on negotiations with the British Free Churches on the basis of the Lambeth Quadrilateral. The latter responded in 1922 by asserting that they could not accept the Creeds as "a sufficient statement of faith" unless they were granted "a reasonable liberty as to their interpretation." As for the historical episcopate and the necessity of episcopal ordination for valid ministry, they countered by demanding recognition of their ministry as valid. At the Joint Conference in 1922 both parties agreed that there is a need for a ministry "acknowledged by every part of the Church as possessing the authority of the whole body," and that the episcopate ought to be accepted "as the means whereby the authority of the whole body is given" in ordination and "ought to be accepted as such for the United Church of the future." Nevertheless, the Anglicans recognized the non-episcopally ordained ministries (Presbyterian and Congregational) as valid and as having been "used and blessed by God," and their polities "as permanent elements in the order and life of the United Church." [6] But this declaration, although signed by distinguished members of the episcopate, was not official or binding on the Church as a whole. The Anglo-Catholics would have rejected it.

All these preparatory developments at last resulted in a major event—the holding of the World Conference on Faith and Order at Lausanne, in August, 1927. This organization was initiated in 1910 by Bishop Charles H. Brent, the first American missionary bishop of the Philippines. He had attended the Edinburgh

[5] James Marchant, ed., *The Reunion of Christendom* (New York, Henry Holt & Company, Inc., 1929), p. 24. Used by permission.

[6] G. K. A. Bell, *Documents on Christian Unity*, First Series (New York, Oxford University Press, 1924), pp. 148–150. Used by permission.

Conference where he had been inspired by the ecumenical vision. Shortly afterward he attended the General Convention of the American Episcopal Church in Cincinnati, where he presented an eloquent plea in behalf of his newly envisioned ecumenical cause. The convention promptly responded by creating a Joint Commission on Faith and Order, of which Robert H. Gardiner became secretary and Bishop Brent a member. This organization aimed at no less a goal than securing doctrinal and polity unity of Christendom. Similar commissions were appointed by other denominations in the United States, Great Britain, and Ireland. And although the two principal ecumenical organizations—Life and Work, and Faith and Order—were conscious of the ultimate identity of their aims, yet at first they went their separate ways. When in 1922 Secretary Gardiner suggested that the two groups meet at the same place and time, Archbishop Söderblom was of the opinion that more effective results could be gained by pursuing their separate goals—the former by securing cooperation of the churches in practical affairs, the latter in working for "the ultimate but more remote goal of unity in Doctrine and Church Order." [7]

Thereupon Brent, at the time Bishop of Western New York, decided to act by calling a Conference on Faith and Order. It was to serve as a wholesome corrective to the overstress on "practical" Christianity which had characterized Stockholm. When it convened in Lausanne, it was attended by 394 delegates from 108 churches, mostly Protestant, with a sprinkling of the Old Catholic and Eastern Orthodox. Among its leaders were Bishop Brent, elected president; Dr. A. E. Garvie, deputy chairman; Archbishop Söderblom; and Otto Dibelius of Berlin. The aim of the leaders, particularly of Bishop Brent, was full organic unity of Christendom. He expressed it in his "Call to Unity," in which he declared: "God has used, beyond anything we had a right to expect, our divided Christendom. But now that we know the sin and disaster of sectarianism, we cannot hope He will use it much longer. . . . It is He who will change for us . . . the impossible into possible, and bring about that

[7] Bell, *The Kingship of Christ*, p. 99.

consummation of Christian hope in a Church that will be one flock under one shepherd." [8] Nevertheless, such a goal at the time proved clearly utopian.

The greatest single achievement of this truly epochal meeting was that it convened at all, for it had been hitherto almost unthinkable that such diverse and estranged elements would consent to exercise sufficient degree of charity to come and reason together. As Bishop Bell expressed it: "The greatest achievement of the Lausanne Conference was to sound the call to unity, and make Christians see its significance." [9] As could have been expected, many far-reaching differences in faith and order readily appeared in the course of discussions, and some proved insurmountable. The Orthodox toward the end almost withdrew, having found themselves too much out of harmony with the rest. They finally reverted to the proposals that had been made by the Ecumenical Patriarch in 1920; namely, that there must first of all be a long preparatory period before reunion could be discussed at all. They voted affirmatively only on one of the reports dealing with the Scriptures. Father Sergius Bulgakov, the most outstanding of the Orthodox theologians, returned from the meeting "grieved and disappointed. When he had raised his voice to defend the veneration of Our Lady . . . the chairman of the meeting would not allow him to speak, and Fr. Sergius felt this as an act of hostility towards the most intimate truth of Orthodoxy." [10] Nevertheless, the greater cause for marvel and satisfaction was the fact that many reports of the commissions were accepted without dissent. There were six points which were presented as the *desiderata* of the united Church and which were approved by the majority: (1) a common faith; (2) baptism as the rite of incorporation into the Church; (3) the holy communion as expressing the corporate life of the Church; (4) ministry recognized by the whole Church; (5) liberty of interpretation regarding the sacramental grace and ministerial

[8] Quoted in Walter Marshall Horton's *Toward a Reborn Church* (New York, Harper & Brothers, 1949), p. 56, n. 2. Used by permission.

[9] Bell, *The Kingship of Christ*, p. 101.

[10] Zander, *op. cit.*, p. 99.

orders; and (6) due provisions for the prophetic gifts. Before the adjournment, a Continuation Committee of thirty-five, among them ten Americans, was elected.

The next important step was the holding of the Oxford-Edinburgh conferences, which by a stroke of ecclesiastical statesmanship on the part of the leaders of the Life and Work and the Faith and Order movements were convened in 1937 a week apart. Prior to the meetings, the Committee of Thirty-five, headed by Dr. William Temple, the Archbishop of York, and charged by both organizations with the duty of preparing recommendations for the forthcoming conferences, had met at Westfield College, London, in July, 1937. They unanimously decided to recommend the uniting of the two organizations into one body—the World Council of Churches, the actual union to be consummated at a later date. The unified body was to continue the respective tasks of the constituent organizations by creating special commissions for that purpose.

The Oxford Conference on Life and Work held its meeting from July 12th to 26th, mainly in the Sheldonian, the Town Hall, St. Mary's Church, and the Christ Church Cathedral. It opened its meetings under the chairmanship of Dr. Cosmo Lang, Archbishop of Canterbury. The delegates comprised most of the outstanding Protestant and Orthodox leaders of the time, although Archbishop Söderblom, the earlier prime mover, was no longer among the living. However, his widow and his son-in-law, Dean Brilioth of the University of Lund, were present. The German Evangelical Church was unable to send any delegates, for it was passing through a period of Nazi persecution and many of its members were imprisoned. Only some German Methodist and Baptist pastors were allowed to attend. The Roman Catholics were represented by unofficial observers. The conference faced problems much graver than its predecessor, the Stockholm Conference, had confronted in 1925; the world situation in 1937 was most serious. The work of the conference was divided into five sections: on Church and Community; on Church and State; on the Economic Order; on Education; and lastly on the Universal Church and the World of Nations.

Perhaps the most important pronouncements were those dealing with Church and State, demanding "that the church should be free to the fullest extent to fulfill its function"; and with the Economic Order, delimiting the rightful functioning of the capitalistic economy and declaring concerning the communist ideology that the Church "cannot surrender to the utopian expectations of these movements and must unequivocally reject their godlessness." But the decision most germane to our purpose was the one regarding the creation of the World Council of Churches. The debate concerning this important step, unanimously recommended by the Committee of Thirty-five, was long and arduous. But when at last the chairman put the question to the vote, it was adopted by the overwhelming majority of 423 against 2.

Eight days later the Conference on Faith and Order opened its sessions in St. Giles Cathedral in Edinburgh. Many delegates to the previous conference at Oxford had also been chosen delegates to Edinburgh. The opening sermon was preached by Archbishop William Temple of York, the successor of Söderblom and others in the leadership of the ecumenical movement, whom Walter M. Horton calls "the Moses of the Movement." He bluntly declared that the division of Christians is "the greatest of all scandals in the face of the world."[11] He was unanimously elected chairman of the conference. The British churches looked upon the problems of "order," that is, ecclesiastical polity, as crucial; the Continental churches, on the other hand, stressed the problem of unity in "faith"; while the American churches emphasized the necessity of cooperative practical work. The agenda was divided into four sections: the Grace of our Lord Jesus Christ; the Word of God and Tradition; Ministry and Sacraments; and lastly Unity in Life and Worship. The aim of the discussions, Archbishop Temple declared, "must be to combine loyalty to the truth we have ourselves received with readiness to learn also the truth which others have received but which we ourselves have either missed

[11] Henry Smith Leiper, *World Chaos or World Christianity* (Chicago, Willett, Clark & Company, 1937), p. 98.

or failed to appreciate in full." [12] Among the Protestant delegates a remarkable degree of unanimity was reached on most of the subjects discussed in the four sections; but this cannot be said about the Orthodox. They reiterated their original stand that if any general agreement is to be reached, much time must be spent in mutual consultation and preliminary conversations, and that the time for conclusions or agreements has not come.

Again as in the case of the Oxford Conference, it was the recommendation of the Committee of Thirty-five which proved to be the culminating point of the deliberations. After another committee, appointed by the Edinburgh Conference, had examined the proposals, they were recommended for adoption. The motion was debated long and even heatedly by the whole assembly: Dr. Headlam, Bishop of Gloucester, made two attempts to secure a negative vote on the ground that the proper task of the Faith and Order organization would be hindered rather than aided by being merged with that of the Life and Work; but he failed to convince the assembly of the validity of his view.[13] The motion to create the World Council of Churches by uniting the two previous movements prevailed by an overwhelming majority. Thereupon, a Continuation Committee was appointed to carry out the details of the formulation of a new provisional body, to be organized definitely at some future time, and the conference closed its memorable sessions with an Act of Thanksgiving.

The provisional status of the World Council of Churches lasted longer than anyone had anticipated. The Second World War had intervened and made the calling of a Constituent Assembly impossible. Nevertheless, many meetings of a preliminary and preparatory character had been held during the eleven years which had elapsed before the Amsterdam Assembly was at last convened at Amsterdam in 1948. The most important of these preliminary meetings was the one convened at Utrecht in 1938 which decided on the draft of the Constitution. As

[12] *Ibid.*, p. 115.
[13] Rouse-Neill, *op. cit.*, p. 434.

everyone knows, at the Amsterdam Assembly the organization of the World Council of Churches was consummated, and its Constitution was adopted without a dissentient vote. Archbishop Temple, who was chairman of the meeting, asked all to stand and implore God for His blessing upon this truly solemn and historic moment, a milestone upon the age-long path of the Christian Church toward the ardently desired goal of Christian unity. But I deliberately refrain from even a cursory description of this meeting, which I hope marks the beginning of a new era in the history of the Church, because I am convinced that such a procedure would be both unnecessary and somewhat insulting as suggesting a widespread nonacquaintance with it on the part of my readers. What I feel *is* necessary, however, is a clarification of the nature and functions of the World Council of Churches. There exists, it seems to me, a really astonishing amount of misconception and of consequent misunderstanding about these matters which imperatively demand to be dealt with. I shall base my analysis on the Constitution of the World Council of Churches as well as on the authoritative interpretation of it by the general secretary of the Council, Dr. Visser 't Hooft.[14]

First of all, he makes clear what the Council is *not*. It is *not* a church, and above all it is not *the* Church—the *Una Sancta*—for, as he writes, "it lacks the essential *notae ecclesiae*." Among the misconceptions prevailing at the time of the Amsterdam Conference, perhaps the most notorious was the one asserted by the Pan-Orthodox Conference of the Eastern Orthodox Churches held in Moscow in 1948. This body rejected the invitation of the Council to accept membership in the body by claiming that the Council aimed at a politically oriented "Ecumenical Church." Among the Moscow pronouncements one reads: "The directing of their [the W.C.C.] efforts into the main stream of social and political life, and the creating of an 'Ecumenical Church' as an important international power, appears to be, as it were, falling into the temptation which was rejected by Christ in the

[14] *Man's Disorder and God's Design* (New York, Harper & Brothers, 1948), I, 177–199. Used by permission.

desert."[15] It is therefore extremely significant that at present Metropolitan Nikolai, after meeting the ranking officials of the World Council of Churches at Utrecht (summer of 1958), declared, "I will report to the Soviet churches, recommending that they join the World Council." This is indeed a reversal of the position taken ten years previously! But even if such a blatant, and in my judgment consciously and deliberately distorted, characterization of the nature and aims of the Council as was expressed at the Moscow Council does not prevail in the West, yet even there it is not always clearly understood that the World Council has not created an ecumenical Church, but is what its name proclaims it to be—the Council of Churches. Visser 't Hooft makes this fact unmistakably evident when he positively declares that the Council is *not* a superchurch, in fact not even a church, and has no authority which the Christian *koinonia,* or *Una Sancta,* would imply. "At the present moment," he writes, "the constitutional limitations of that authority are probably more rigid than those placed on any other representative church body in the world. Now these limitations are inevitable and even desirable under present conditions. . . . But that fact by itself shows that the World Council is by no means a first preliminary edition of the Una Sancta." In another authoritative document, this subject is further amplified to the effect that the "Assembly and Central Committee will have no constitutional authority whatever over its constituent churches. . . . Not only has the Council no power to legislate for the participating churches; it is also forbidden to act in their name except in so far as all or any of them have commissioned it to do so."[16]

But on the other hand, Visser 't Hooft denies that the World Council is a mere organization, and declares that it "cannot be satisfied with that role." The only reason he adduces for this view is that "it cannot be a mere organization because it is a Council of *Churches*. For the Church in the churches insists on

[15] *Proceedings of the Conference of Heads and Representatives of Autocephalous Orthodox Churches* (Paris, YMCA Press, 1951), p. 240. Used by permission.

[16] *The World Council of Churches: Its Process of Formation* (Geneva, World Council of Churches, 1946), p. 182. Used by permission.

asserting itself. Whenever two or three churches are gathered together, the Una Sancta is in the midst of them and demands to be manifested." This is not only a questionable use of Scriptural quotation, but is disturbing as indicating an instability of the present organization of the World Council.

What then *is* the World Council? The Constitution defines its nature and functions by asserting: (1) that its work is that of carrying on the functions of the two original constituent bodies—the Life and Work and the Faith and Order movements; (2) that it aims to facilitate common action on the part of the churches; (3) that it promotes cooperative study; (4) that it fosters the growth of ecumenical consciousness; (5) that it establishes relations with denominational federations and other ecumenical movements; (6) and finally that it has the function of calling world conferences. Visser 't Hooft further amplifies this description by saying that the Council serves "as a means to manifest the unity of the Church, whenever and wherever the Lord of the Church Himself gives that unity; a *means* and a *method* and no more. The World Council *is* not the Una Sancta, but a means and a method which have no other *raison d'être* than to be used for the building of the Una Sancta."[17] Thus the Council in his view points beyond itself, and as such is only a provisional organization.

Membership in the World Council is restricted to churches (a term which is broadly construed) represented by their *official* delegates. The only doctrinal requirement for membership is the acceptance of "our Lord Jesus Christ as God and Saviour." This phrase has a curious history: it was taken over verbatim from the Faith and Order Movement, which in turn had derived it from the Paris Basis of the Y.M.C.A. (1855). The formula is radically faulty from the theological point of view, since it is manifestly monophysite; but it is *not* an incipient creedal statement. The Council "does not concern itself with the manner in which the churches interpret" this formula, as the minutes of the Provisional Committee at its 1946 meeting inform us.[18] Accordingly, it is not even intended to be a unifying principle;

[17] *Man's Disorder,* I, 187.
[18] *The World Council of Churches: Its Process of Formation,* p. 182.

to think that it represents a basic declaration of unity in doctrine is obviously an error, and the fact that it does not is comforting. Outler calls it "a pre-theological standpoint,"[19] for a creed acceptable to all cannot as yet be attempted. But even so, that does not justify the choosing of a faulty phrase.

To sum up then: by its Constitution the World Council of Churches has made it perfectly clear that it is a Council of *Churches*—not a church or superchurch, and least of all not the *Una Sancta* itself. The constituent bodies have surrendered nothing of their autonomous character in faith and order. They have remained independent of each other as they had been before entering the Council. Later developments made this autonomy even more startlingly and starkly evident, as when at the meeting of the Central Committee held at Toronto in July, 1950, the principle was adopted that "the member churches of the World Council of Churches do not necessarily recognize each other as true, healthy or complete churches, but they consider the relation of *other* churches to the Una Sancta as a question for mutual consideration."[20] The Orthodox churches at Amsterdam and ever since have certainly spared no effort and have left nothing undone or unsaid to make it clear that only they constitute the true Church—and none besides them. We shall return to this aspect of the case later. Furthermore, the Council cannot take any action binding upon its member churches or make any pronouncement in their name; it may only formulate proposals and suggestions, but must leave it to its constituent bodies to accept, ignore, or reject them. Thus when the Toronto meeting adopted resolutions condemning the Nazis, Lutherans promptly protested. For the same reason communism cannot be officially condemned in explicit terms—the churches behind the Iron Curtain would instantly and vigorously oppose it. Conversely, actions of the member churches do not reflect upon, or become the responsibility of, the Council itself.

Such being the case, no wonder that many thoroughgoing

[19] Albert C. Outler, *The Christian Tradition and the Unity We Seek* (New York, Oxford University Press, 1957), p. 97. Used by permission.

[20] Quoted in Outler, *op. cit.*, pp. 98–99.

ecumenicists have been secretly or openly disappointed with the Council of Churches and look upon it as only the initial stage—or the means toward the real goal—of the *Una Sancta,* the One, Holy, Catholic, and Apostolic Church. Thus the age-long aspiration of the Christian churches does not find an adequate realization in the stage we have thus far reached. Nor will the World Council serve as "the means and method" toward that goal unless its present Constitution is radically subverted, for it is a federation of *churches,* and its constituent bodies are by no means ready to surrender their separate identities. Thus its own claim to ecumenicity (symbolized by the official device incorporating the word *oikumene*) is, on a strict construction of the term, at least pretentious, if not unjustified.

Accordingly, there exist two parties within the movement: within the Council itself many member churches and their official representatives are committed to the federative character of that body as to all intents and purposes its permanent stage and form, and except for improvements of its present essential structure desire no change; in fact, they would oppose such a change on principle. Some of them, for instance the Lutherans, expressed themselves, even at Utrecht in 1938, in no uncertain terms that they would withdraw from the Council were its present federative character as a Council of *Churches* subverted in favor of one all-inclusive Church, particularly if it were to take the form of organic union, instead of unity which implies no uniformity in doctrine and polity. We may speak of these, for want of a better term, as federalists or conciliarists, adherents and supporters of the federative principle embodied in the World Council of Churches. I am glad to find myself supported in this characterization of the two parties within the Council by Walter M. Horton, who designated those who desired to retain the federative nature of the movement as "minimalists or Mensheviki."[21]

But there also exist both within and outside the Council those who take the specifically declared goal of the ultimate realization of the *Una Sancta* most seriously, and who regard the

[21] Horton, *op. cit.,* p. 91.

Council as the provisional means toward that end. It is this group to which I refer as the ecumenicists, and I use the term without any pejorative intent, but purely in a descriptive sense. Horton refers to this party as "the maximalists, or to translate this term into Russian, the ecclesiastical Bolsheviki," and declares himself to be "a maximalist Bolshevik" as far as the ultimate nature of the Church is concerned, although a Menshevik in his "conception of the kind of ecclesiastical authority the Ecumenical Church should exercise over its members." [22] He forgot that a Russian could not be a Bolshevik and a Menshevik at the same time, and that the former had ruthlessly exterminated the latter. This maximalist position is validated by the official pronouncements of Visser 't Hooft and numberless others. In other words, a sharp distinction must be drawn between those who of set conviction adhere to the present Constitution of the World Council as to all intents and purposes permanent, and those who are striving through the Council as their provisional instrument to attain the ultimate goal of the *Una Sancta*. For weal or woe, this treatment is devoted principally to the latter group. It is therefore inevitable that what is said about the ecumenicists need not necessarily apply to, and may even contradict the thinking of, convinced federalists. But whatever worth this treatment may have, it at least should make clear the existence of these two groups and forces within the ecumenical movement, and bring their reciprocal relations into a sharper focus.

Furthermore, as in every other movement, there exists a large body of well-wishers, professed adherents, or even official members of the Council and its various affiliates who occupy a middle position. They are neither convinced federalists nor declared ecumenicists. Perhaps they are not even aware of the conflicting or mutually exclusive principles of the two parties. But whatever is the reason for their middle stand, they belong to neither group.

Accordingly, we must pursue the subject beyond the stage reached by the World Council and observe the avowed aims

[22] *Ibid.*, pp. 91, 92.

of the ecumenicists in greater detail. We enter upon a bewildering confusion of voices, all clamoring for the *Una Sancta,* but widely differing among themselves as to the nature of the goal and the means of attaining it. Any attempt at a truly comprehensive description of this multiplicity of proposals would require several volumes. I shall merely touch upon some of them in order to point out the chaotic stage in which these aspirations at present appear and to suggest the necessity of clarification.

To begin with, let us take the term "ecumenical." It was chosen not so much because it differed essentially from the usual word "catholic," that is, general or universal (although some Eastern Orthodox do put upon it a different connotation by the Russian term *soborny*), but as the less likely to be confused with the exclusive and proprietary claims made upon that term principally by the Roman Catholic and Eastern Orthodox churches. The term "ecumenical" necessarily connotes the unitary nature of the Christian Church: the Church is One. Both terms, then, "catholic" and "ecumenical," cannot be properly applied to any but the whole Church of Christ existing throughout the world. If this self-evident connotation of the term needs to be supported, I may refer to the characterization of Walter M. Horton, who declares, "In plain English, the Ecumenical Movement is a *movement toward one universal Christian Church 'throughout the whole inhabited world.'* "[23] Accordingly, it must comprise all existing Christian communions—that is, the Roman Catholic, Eastern Orthodox, Protestant, and any other which may rightfully claim the generic term Christian, for instance to the fifteen millions of the non-Chalcedonian Christians of India and elsewhere. Presumably, the majority of ecumenicists, compelled by the logic of the situation either clearly envisaged or dimly adumbrated, think in these all-inclusive terms, despite the manifest impossibility of devising any comprehensive scheme for effecting such a union. So far no one, to my best knowledge, has been seriously advocating that the Protestant or Orthodox communions surrender unconditional-

[23] *Ibid.,* p. 9.

ally to the supreme authority of the pope as the vicar of Christ, or that we Protestants accept the exclusive claims of Eastern Orthodoxy to being the only true Church of Christ. Some, recoiling from this logical conclusion, desperately hold on to the rather faint hope that the Roman Catholics and Eastern Orthodox might in time change their minds; hence they advocate "keeping the door open" for such an unlikely eventuality. Thus for instance Walter M. Horton writes that the Council serves as a framework within which "the ancient Catholic-Protestant antithesis can be wrestled with until it is finally transcended in a great Church as universal as the Catholic ideal requires and as free Protestant ideal demands." [24] How these two ecclesiastical traditions can "wrestle" within the Council when one of them categorically refuses to enter into the Council he does not explain. Bishop Angus Dun, in his book *Prospecting for a United Church,* also betrays a faint hope of the ultimate inclusion of the Roman Catholic Church in the ecumenical Church. He writes that the truly united Church "is very far off. To those of us who stand outside of Roman Catholicism, it appears that that great church remains immovable—stiffening, it would seem, and becoming less approachable." [25] And yet, he recognizes that without it there can be "no truly unified church." Canon Theodore O. Wedel, a brilliant and eloquent protagonist of organic union, in his book *The Coming Great Church* is even less hopeful of inclusion of the Roman Catholic Church in the ecumenical body. He writes:

> I join my Protestant brethren in the belief that the Reformation is still the greatest recovery of the Gospel in Christian history since the New Testament itself. If this Gospel should be endangered by sympathetic consideration of the Church life on the other side of the chasm [the Roman Catholic side], we had best leave historic Catholicism strictly alone.[26]

[24] *Ibid.*, 93.

[25] Angus Dun, *Prospecting for a United Church* (New York, Harper & Brothers, 1948), p. 26. Used by permission.

[26] Theodore O. Wedel, *The Coming Great Church* (New York, The Macmillan Company, 1945), p. 82. Used by permission.

But then the Coming Great Church so ardently desired by Dr. Wedel would obviously not be ecumenical. Perhaps the most vigorous and uninhibited critique of practically all other views of "ecumenicity" is to be found in the several volumes which Dr. C. C. Morrison has devoted to this subject. In his latest, entitled *The Unfinished Reformation,* he declares that there exist

> profound and irreconcilable differences between Protestantism and Roman Catholicism. It is one thing to "leave the door open" to the participation of the Roman Church in this movement, and quite another thing to cherish any expectation that the invitation will be accepted. And it is still less realistic to allow so remote a possibility to affect either the conception or the planning of a union of the non-Roman churches. It is little short of a betrayal of the ecumenical aspiration to inhibit its progress and realization in American Protestantism by complicating the problem with any hint that Protestant action should be slowed down in any degree by the fatuous hope of cooperation on the part of the Roman Church.[27]

He further declares:

> The differences between Roman Catholicism and Protestantism are crucial and insoluble short of radical transformation of one or the other. Therefore, to be diverted from our search for Protestant unity by a sentimental consideration of reconciliation with Roman Catholicism would be like dropping the bone to seize the shadow.[28]

These four outstanding ecumenicists, then, range in their concepts from an avowed hope of including Roman Catholicism (in all four instances the Eastern Orthodox are not even mentioned) to its complete exclusion, and their views represent only a small sampling of the prevailing variety. But what then becomes of the goal of the *Una Sancta* properly conceived? Perhaps these few examples will suffice to prove the need of clarification of the term. The present usage is with rare exceptions nebulous and therefore misleading.

[27] C. C. Morrison, *The Unfinished Reformation* (New York, Harper & Brothers, 1953), p. 104. Used by permission.
[28] *Ibid.,* p. xii.

A similar chaotic welter of conflicting opinions characterizes the means toward the attainment of the ecumenical goal. Some advocate the restoration of the primitive apostolic conditions or at the most the conditions prevailing during the first five centuries of the Christian era. The vast majority of others think in terms of integrating the distinctive elements of each doctrinal, ecclesiastical, or denominational tradition into one whole, thus creating a huge conglomeration of heterogeneous traditions, reminding one of Dostoevski's unity of an ant heap. Others think that only a clean sweep of the past, and a new start, would give us the unity we seek. We must return to a more detailed discussion of these proposals later. The astonishing sweep of these various proposals may be seen in the case of Dr. Morrison, a Disciple, who has advanced from the restorationist proposals traditional in his fellowship to the repudiation of all existing "churches" as sects. A sect assumes prerogatives which belong only to the Church—administration of sacraments, ordination, missions, worship, creeds, polity. This usurpation is sinful, the sin of "churchism," as he calls it. He logically insists on the sin's complete annihilation and extinction. He writes that the ecumenical Church and denominational sects "are mutually exclusive. If we have denominational churches, we cannot have the ecumenical church. And, *vice versa,* if we are to have the ecumenical church, we cannot have denominational churches." [29]

But unfortunately for this theory, there exists at present no ecumenical Church of Christ, or as Dr. Morrison puts it, it is

> an amorphous thing. We cannot see it. We cannot lay hold of it. It eludes our grasp. Nor can it lay hold of us to draw us into itself. The Church of Christ is, we might say, a phantom church. . . . It is this amorphous character of the Church of Christ, its formlessness, its intangibleness, its invisibility and its empirical impotence that the ecumenical movement is to overcome.[30]

In short, the Church of Christ does not really exist; it must still be created. Thus, strangely enough in Morrison's proposal the

[29] *Ibid.,* p. 54.
[30] *Ibid.*

extremes meet: he is an unequivocal advocate of a "superchurch"! But who, then, is to perform the functions of the Church before it is created?

Somewhat less extreme is the proposal of another outstanding Disciple and a leader in the ecumenical movement, Winfred E. Garrison. In his latest book he takes his fellow ecumenicists severely to task for beating their breasts and loudly professing repentance for "the sin of division" and then returning home from their ecumenical meetings and blithely going on sinning. His solution is a simple one: in his judgment "the diversity of opinion in doctrine, polity, and orders is not itself sinful; . . . division in the Church is sinful." [31] To his mind, the essential unity is neither institutional nor doctrinal, but spiritual, consisting in common loyalty to Christ as Lord. Hence, all that needs to be done is "to unite as quickly and fully as possible with all other Christians regardless of the differences which have sinfully been made the grounds of separation from them." [32] It is as radical and as simple as that! But what of those who would not unite on these terms? The author advises us to leave them alone until they change their mind, which confessedly would take a long, long time. Would they ever join on these terms? I doubt it. So it appears to be too soon to talk about the "united Church," and least of all of "ecumenicity."

I hope this demonstrates sufficiently clearly that the ecumenicists are far apart in their thinking regarding both the goal of their quest and the means of attaining it. At the present time, if the diverse plans were by some miracle to be realized, they would create not one, but a large number of "ecumenical churches," which would be warring with each other not a whit less than the existing unreconciled ones. In the next two chapters let us seek to make clear, on the basis of more detailed but by no means comprehensive examination, what the quest would probably imply as far as the necessary reconstruction in doctrine and polity is concerned. The last chapter then will be devoted

[31] Winfred E. Garrison, *The Quest and Character of a United Church* (New York, Abingdon Press, 1957), p. 216. Used by permission.

[32] *Ibid.*, p. 217.

to an evaluation of the positive and concrete elements of this potentially the most important and beneficial movement of our times. This attempt will seek to divest it of the irresponsible sentimentalism which has often characterized the movement, and to propose a realistic approach to the quest for unity.

CHAPTER II

WHAT PRICE THEOLOGICAL SYNTHESIS?

The conclusion of the previous chapter has left little hope that the grandiose dream of a united Christendom can at present—if ever—be fully realized. The absolute claims of the Roman Catholic and Orthodox churches obtrude what appears as insurmountable difficulties. Yet it would be premature to regard such conclusions as proved. We must first of all examine these formidable obstacles in greater detail. Until that is done, and a conclusion is reached which is based on factual grounds, I propose to deal with the ecumenical aspirations in their maximal scope.

As the report of the Amsterdam Assembly itself has pointed out, the "deepest differences" among Christian churches exist in the realm of ecclesiology. At Lund (1952) it became apparent that what Outler calls "the ecumenical honeymoon" was over, and that the "hard-core disagreements" could not be solved. "As things now stand," he writes, "our existing disagreements on the doctrines of church, ministry, and sacraments are 'insoluble.'"[1] It is really strange that the doctrine of the Church should have been so grievously neglected throughout Christian history. To be sure, there are many other grave issues as yet unresolved; but most of them are organically connected with the view one takes of the Church, and their solution depends on what conclusion one

[1] Outler, *The Christian Tradition . . .*, pp. 6, 8.

adopts. Furthermore, these "deepest differences" concern what is theologically known as the "Church visible," that is, the historical and institutional ecclesiastical organizations as they have developed separately during the past almost two millennia. Had the concept of the "Church invisible" been taken seriously by the ecumenicists, most of their difficulties would have been greatly minimized or have vanished altogether. As understood since the days of St. Augustine, the Church at its core and in its essence is the body of Christ conceived as a communion of saints or the totality of the predestinate. All others are indeed in the Church but are not of the Church. This concept was revived by Wyclif and Hus—for whom even the pope need not necessarily have been one of the predestinate—and later by the Reformers—Luther, Calvin, and others. Under the term *sobornost* it was held even by the Father of the Russian Renascence, Alexey S. Khomyakov, and his school, including Bulgakov and other modern Russian theologians. We may express the basic idea by saying, "Where Christ is there is the Church," or "He who has not the Spirit of Christ is none of His." It is only in accordance with this concept that we may say that the Church is One. It certainly is not one when considered from the point of view of "visible" churches; or why should there exist an ecumenical movement having for its aim unity of these separated bodies?

Unfortunately, this concept of the "Church invisible" does not satisfy the ecumenicists, and some reject it altogether. They insist on bringing about unity of the Church visible, and that is a different matter altogether! For if by the definition given above, the visible Church consists of both those who possess the Spirit of Christ and those who do not, no external organizational device will eliminate and overcome this basic difference. Only an inner change wrought by the Holy Spirit in the hearts of the latter group can make unity possible.

Accordingly, the principal confusion in the concepts of the Church inheres in identifying the outward organization of the Church with the body of Christ. This is done by the Roman Catholic Church, which makes the exclusive claim to be the only true Church, outside of which there is no salvation. In his encyclical *Immortale Dei* (1885) Pope Leo XIII asserted that Christ gave the Church "unrestrained authority in regard to things sacred . . . with the power of making laws, as also with the twofold right of judging and punishing, which flow from that power." "It is the Church, and not the State, that is to be man's guide to Heaven. It is to the Church that God has assigned the charge of seeing to and legislating for all that concerns religion . . . of administering freely and without hindrance, in accordance with her own judgement, all matters that fall within her own competence."[2] Leo here clearly asserts that he, as the vicar of Christ, yields this "unrestrained authority in regard to things sacred" which Christ has granted the Church, so that in a manner of speaking He, Christ, no longer rules the Church, but the Church rules in His stead. This is putting the Church in the place of Christ—a thing utterly inadmissible. Furthermore, as Pope Pius XI further defined this power in his encyclical *Mortalium animos* (1928), "Christ founded His Church as a perfect society, of its nature external and perceptible by the senses, which in the future should carry on the work of salvation of mankind under one head, with a living teaching authority, administering the sacraments which are the source of heavenly grace. . . ."[3] The only possible method of reunion is by "the return to the one true Church of Christ." For, as the pope continues,

How can men with opposite convictions belong to one and the same federation of the faithful: those who accept sacred Tradition as a source of revelation and those who reject it; those who recognize as divinely constituted the hierarchy of bishops, priests, and ministers in the Church, and those who regard it as gradually introduced to suit the conditions of the time; those who adore Christ really present in the Most Holy Eucharist through that wonderful conversion of the bread and wine, transubstantiation, and those who assert that the body of Christ is there only by faith or by the signification and virtue of the sacrament; those who in

[2] Philip Hughes, *The Popes' New Order* (New York, The Macmillan Company, 1944), p. 92. Used by permission.

[3] Marchant, ed., *The Reunion of Christendom,* p. 15.

the Eucharist recognize both sacrament and sacrifice, and those who say that it is nothing more than the memorial of the Lord's supper; those who think it right and useful to pray to the Saints reigning with Christ, especially to Mary the Mother of God, and to venerate their images, and those who refuse such veneration as derogatory to the honor due to Jesus Christ, "the one mediator of God and men." [4]

Pope Pius XII asserted in an encyclical that after Christ's ascension the Church builds not only on Christ but on Peter, His viceroy, as well, so that both must be regarded as constituting one head of the Church.[5]

These Roman Catholic absolute and exclusive claims are fairly well known, and their overweening pretensions, particularly as to the papal powers and the pope's vicarship in place of Christ, generally rejected by Protestants and Orthodox alike; but it is not sufficiently realized that the Eastern Orthodox are equally adamant in similar, although not all, respects. Professor Georges Florovsky, the widely known Russian Orthodox theologian, published an article after the Amsterdam Conference in which he explains the reason why he regards the eventual union of Christendom as impossible except on the Orthodox terms. The Orthodox Church, he declares, is "the sole true Church," "the universal truth, truth for the entire world, for all times and all people." [6] And further in the "Declaration of the Orthodox Delegates concerning the Report on Faith and Order" issued at the Evanston Conference of the World Council of Churches, the Orthodox declared that

when we are considering the problem of Church unity, we cannot envisage it in any other way than as the complete restoration of the total faith and the total Episcopal structure of the Church which is basic to the sacramental life of the Church. We would not pass judgment upon those of the separated communions. However, it is our conviction that in these communions certain basic elements are lacking which constitute

[4] *Ibid.*, pp. 21–22.

[5] K. E. Skydsgaard, *One in Christ* (Philadelphia, Muhlenberg Press, 1957), p. 105. Used by permission.

[6] Irénikon (Chevetogne, Belgium, Prieuré Bénédictin d'Amay), xxii (1949), No. 1, pp. 9–10.

the reality of the fulness of the Church. We believe that the return of the communions to the Faith of the ancient, united and indivisible Church of the Seven Ecumenical Councils, namely to the pure and unchanged and common heritage of the forefathers of all divided Christians, shall alone produce the desired re-union of all separated Christians. For, only the unity and the fellowship of Christians in a common Faith shall have as a necessary result their fellowship in the sacraments and their indissoluble unity in love, as members of one and the same Body of the one Church of Christ. . . . In conclusion, we are bound to declare our profound conviction that the Holy Orthodox Church alone has preserved in full and intact "the faith once delivered to the saints." [7]

This is certainly plain speaking which should have left no one in the slightest doubt as to where these two historic communions, comprising the majority of Christians, stand in relation to the ecumenical movement. But they are not the only ones making such exclusive claims: Southern Baptists and Missouri Synod Lutherans, not to mention a large number of numerically insignificant "splinter groups" or "fringe bodies," take the same intransigent attitude. To slightly less degree many Anglicans share this view by recognizing as "branches" of the true Church only the Roman Catholics and Orthodox, along with themselves, but refusing to include any of the non-episcopal churches. In accordance with this clearly defined position, the Roman Catholics logically refuse to take part in ecumenical "conversations," in fact are forbidden to do so. Cardinal Bourne of Westminster wrote in regard to it that "to a Catholic such a conception of Unity [as the ecumenicists hold] is not only repugnant but quite impossible." [8] Some Eastern Orthodox indeed cooperate—the late Archbishop Michael, Exarch of the Ecumenical Patriarch in North and South America, one of the presidents of the Central Committee of the World Council of Churches, and afterMichael's death, his successor, the Archbishop James, a member of the Central Committee—but such participation is conceived strictly as a witness to the Truth borne to the

[7] *St. Vladimir's Seminary Quarterly* (New York, St. Vladimir's Orthodox Theological Seminary), Fall, 1954–Winter, 1955, pp. 20–21.

[8] Marchant, ed., *op. cit.*, p. 3.

separated brethren with the view to bring them back into the bosom of the one true Church of Christ. This statement has been repeated with exemplary steadfastness and inexhaustible patience by Orthodox delegations at practically all ecumenical gatherings; hence, there should exist no substantial doubt as to the serious nature of the purpose thus expressed.

In view of these positive declarations on the part of the two great Christian communions, which amount to a rejection of the ecumenical aims except on their own terms, what attitude do the Protestant churches, or rather the ecumenicists within them, assume? Do they accept them at their face value as rejections? Do they conclude, regretfully but nonetheless realistically, that any further efforts to induce these communions to regard the Protestant churches on equality with themselves as vain? Do they realize that by futilely reaching after the moon they are frustrating the chances of their own unitive efforts? Curiously, these are not the conclusions of the majority, especially vis-à-vis the Eastern Orthodox. Discouraged though they must be in the face of repeated failures to gain at least a degree of mutual recognition as members of the Church of Christ, they bravely press on with their grandiose and all-inclusive project. Their theologians are still busy devising theological syntheses attempting to comprehend what is at present quite incomprehensible. They are engaged in doing for the Roman Catholics and Eastern Orthodox what these communions categorically refuse to do for themselves—delimiting or even rejecting their various dogmas and doctrines to make them acceptable to all, including themselves. Some even talk of "leaving the door open," so that at some future time of the hoped-for spiritual "Big Thaw," when these communions have had a chance to think it over in a repentant or chastened mood, they might perhaps join us! Surely it must sound preposterous—or should I say fantastic?—to the two self-sufficient communions! But as long as such comprehensive schemes or accommodations are being produced and seriously propounded, we must include them in our consideration.

In attempting to present these various and often discordant

schemes in some orderly fashion, I have organized them in an integrated form without following any particular current or individual pattern. For this purpose I have adopted a historic formula devised by a relatively obscure German Protestant pastor of the post-Reformation era, Peter Meiderlin; *"In necessariis unitas; in dubiis libertas; in omnibus caritas."* Or, to put it in a modern form: "In essentials unity; in non-essentials liberty; and in all things love." I assume that modern Protestants would find no fault with the principle, even though they are likely to differ in its interpretation. The Eastern Orthodox in their formal dogmatic treatises make a similar distinction between dogmas—officially adopted by the seven ecumenical councils; *theologumena,* which consist of theological opinions of the Fathers of the Church, whose authority is great, although not absolute; and, finally, private views or opinions of theologians not binding on anyone and permitted to be held freely, unless they should contradict Scripture or tradition or the above-mentioned categories. The infallible interpreter of all doctrine is the Church. Stefan Zankov writes about this matter: "Dogma is the true doctrine, fixed by an Oecumenical Council and accepted by the whole Church: only a thesis so determined has the obligatory character of a dogma. . . . Besides these must be considered the 'theologumena' of the Church Fathers and propositions of Orthodox theological science." [9] In a recent conference with the Anglicans, the Russian Orthodox declared: "Dogmas are binding and necessary because their significance is absolute; the acceptance and profession of them is a necessary condition of our salvation. . . . They are the voice, the teaching of God Himself in Holy Scripture and Holy tradition." [10] An illustration of a "private opinion" may be seen in the "sophiology" originally propounded by Vladimir Solovev and developed by his disciple Sergius Bulgakov, formerly dean of the Russian Theological

[9] Stefan Zankov, *The Eastern Orthodox Church* (Milwaukee, Morehouse-Gorham Co., Inc., 1929), pp. 39–40. Used by permission.

[10] H. M. Waddams, ed., *Anglo-Russian Theological Conference* (London, Faith Press, Ltd., 1957), pp. 37–38. Used by permission.

Institute in Paris. Despite its condemnation (partly for political reasons) by the late Patriarch Sergius of the Russian Orthodox Church, this opinion is still held by some contemporaneous Russian theologians.

On this basis, the only dogmas actually determined by the ecumenical councils are two in number: the Trinity and the two natures of Jesus Christ. The councils of Nicaea (325) and I Constantinople (381) defined the Trinitarian formula, which is thus of dogmatic authority. There are several possible interpretations of the dogma of the One God (*ousia*) in three of His divine manifestations or revelations (*hypostases*); these differing interpretations are permitted, provided they do not negate the dogma itself. It also necessarily implies the doctrine of Incarnation, that is, that one of these three divine revelations is to be identified with the Word Who became flesh and dwelt among us in the person of Jesus Christ. Accordingly, this amounts to a dogmatic definition and is, therefore, essential to the Christian faith. The other dogmatic definition was adopted by the Council of Chalcedon (451) and deals with the relation of the human and divine natures in Jesus Christ without destroying the unity of His person. The remaining three councils acknowledged by the Eastern Orthodox have added nothing essential to the dogmatic teaching and need not be considered. The dogmas mentioned above are, therefore, of the essence of the faith, and as such have formed, for some sixteen centuries, the dogmatic kernel of historic Christianity.

This position is essentially similar to what is known as the "canon" of Vincent of Lérins, defining the Catholic faith as that which has been believed *quod ubique et semper et ab omnibus*—everywhere, always, and by all.[11] The canon ignores the fact that the final definition of the above-mentioned dogmas required from three to four centuries to reach that form, and thus that they were not believed "always" nor by "all." But with a little conscious generosity of latitude we might let it pass.

But despite the Vincentian canon, presumably held by the Roman Catholics, the case is very different with the gradually

[11] *Patrologia latina,* v. 50, col. 610.

highly developed dogmatic system of that body. For one thing, they have interpolated into the Niceno-Constantinopolitan Creed the *Filioque* clause, asserting that the Holy Spirit proceeds from the Father *and the Son.* This distortion of the original version has ever been regarded by the Orthodox East as a grave departure from the dogmatic purity of the faith and therefore a heresy, and the controversy has by no means been resolved to this day. But perhaps this is partly a dogmatic rationalization of the deep-seated resentment of the East to the absolutely unjustifiable Fourth Crusade (1204) of which Runciman declares: "There was never a greater crime against humanity than the 4th Crusade." [12] But furthermore, the Roman Catholic Church proceeded to make dogmatic pronouncements after 787 when the Seventh Ecumenical Council, recognized as the last of the united Church, was held. The Orthodox, therefore, refuse to recognize as ecumenical any of the remaining thirteen councils held in the West. They declare that some of the decisions proclaimed by these additional councils were erroneous or even heretical. Furthermore, down to the twentieth of the Roman Catholic councils—the Vatican Council of 1870—the Roman Catholics asserted that dogmatic decisions must rest on Scripture and tradition and must be adopted by general councils. But this rule was broken for the first time in 1854 when Pope Pius IX, without convoking a council and on his own authority, proclaimed the Immaculate Conception of the Virgin as a dogma, although it had no Scriptural basis. In the same way, in 1870, he proclaimed on his own authority (although in that instance a general council was actually in session) the dogma of papal infallibility. He made the declaration on the basis of his own inherent power, merely with the "concurrence" of the council. This, too, lacked a Scriptural basis. Moreover, it basically changed the nature of the Roman Church, since henceforth general councils are no longer necessary and none has since been called, although the present pope, John XXIII, is convoking one. The late pope, Pius XII, speaking for the first time ex

[12] Steven Runciman, *A History of the Crusades* (Cambridge and New York, Cambridge University Press, 1954), III, 130. Used by permission.

cathedra, exercised his prerogative by proclaiming, in 1950, the dogma of the physical Assumption of the Virgin—which is quite an assumption! All these three latest dogmas rest solely upon tradition—the dogmatic decision of the Council of Trent, that the sources of authority are Scripture and tradition, having been thus disregarded. Accordingly, they represent, in my judgment, an insurmountable barrier to the hopes of any future union, being rejected by Protestants and Orthodox alike. Since it is necessary for salvation that Roman Catholics accept and heartily hold all dogmas proclaimed as of the essence of the Faith by the infallible pope, it is inconceivable that any of them would ever be repealed. In fact, there exists a strong likelihood that other dogmas—particularly such as would further the Marian cult—would be proclaimed in the future.

The attitude of the Orthodox to these latest Roman Catholic dogmatic developments is well summarized by a contemporary Russian Orthodox theologian, L. A. Zander. He points out that the dogma of papal infallibility holds the supreme rank in the whole Roman system. For in it are subsumed all other doctrinal articles, since in the infallible pope

> all questions of faith receive their infallible and final interpretation. Submission to the Pope is therefore absolute, and means a renunciation of one's reason and will in the deepest, metaphysical sense of the term. It is perfectly comprehensible that the Catholic Church can confine itself to these two demands [truths *de fide divina et de fide ecclesiastica* and papal infallibility]: all the rest—forms, rites, sacraments, church administrations, questions of spiritual discipline, of religious philosophy—have no decisive significance. . . . In view of this the Roman Catholic Church can admit much variety and be extremely plastic. But all this freedom . . . exists *intra muros* and *cum permissu superiorum*.[13]

As for the Protestants, it is clear that to accept the claims of Roman Catholicism would be tantamount to a denial of the Reformation itself and the loss of their hard-won religious freedoms. If any Protestant ecumenicist is willing and ready to pay this price, I have not yet learned of it. For myself I regard

[13] Zander, *Vision and Action*, pp. 170–171.

such a surrender as unthinkable. If the ecumenical movement should develop in such a direction and involve the virtual surrender to the claims of Rome on the part of both the Orthodox and the Protestants, it would cease to be ecumenical: it would be an act of absorption, not of union.

What then of the Protestant position on this most important matter of the unity in the essentials of the Christian faith? Ever since the Reformation, irenic theologians of the type of Georg Calixtus have advocated the *consensus quinque saecularis*—acceptance of the dogmas adopted by the first four ecumenical councils—a favorite formula of some modern ecumenicists as well. But more recently and concretely, this proposal is included in the Lambeth Quadrilateral, in terms of recognition of Scripture of the Old and New Testaments as the supreme rule of faith and morals, and the Apostles' and the Nicene creeds as sufficient statements of faith. Subjected to a thoroughgoing discussion at the various conferences on Faith and Order and other similar gatherings of less official character, this formulation was approved with certain reservations guarding a reasonable freedom of interpretation both of the Bible and of the creeds. Classical treatises on the doctrinal systems of the Reformation—conspicuously Calvin's *Institutes*—although proclaiming Scripture as the supreme rule, understood the concept broadly as including the doctrinal developments of the first five centuries. The Apostles' Creed actually forms the basic pattern of Calvin's *Institutes,* and the same is true of some Reformation catechisms. It appears therefore safe to say that most Protestants would find the proposed dogmatic basis quite acceptable, even though the liberal-minded would insist on freedom in rejecting or modifying such expressions as the descent into hell, the Virgin birth, and the resurrection of flesh. Moreover, Protestants have somewhat incautiously adopted the Roman Catholic version of the Nicene Creed, including the *Filioque* clause. At the Anglo-Russian Theological Conference held in Moscow in July, 1956, the Orthodox again declared that the condemnation of the *Filioque* clause is "an absolute condition of union." The Anglicans, although admitting the absence of the phrase from the original text of the Niceno-Constantinopolitan Creed, were not ready to accede to the demand of the Orthodox.[14] This matter should perhaps be reconsidered by the Protestants in the light of the original version.

A really curious feature of the Protestant formulation of the essentials in faith in its official versions is that it omits any reference to the Chalcedonian Creed. Accordingly, it differs from the Orthodox in including the Apostles' Creed (which the latter do not mention) but not including the Chalcedonian Creed (which they do mention). There is no doubt in my mind that the vast majority of Protestants accept the dogma of the two natures of our Lord (despite the strange fact that the formula required of all churches seeking membership in the World Council of Churches omits any mention of the human nature of Jesus). Is this noninclusion of the Chalcedonian formula an oversight? Whatever the reason for it, the fact remains that it is omitted from the official Protestant formulations of the essentials of the Christian faith.

There is one further consideration apropos the Chalcedonian Creed: It contains the unfortunate term *Theotokos*—properly translated as the God-bearer, but erroneously rendered as the Mother of God. This term has proved the source of Mariology throughout the subsequent Christian era. In accepting the Chalcedonian Creed for the rightful and acknowledged dogmatic formulation of the two natures in one person in Jesus Christ, Protestants must beware of becoming unwittingly entangled in the questionable peripheral doctrine concerning the *Theotokos*.

This, I hope, affords us an idea of what the ecumenical theologian is confronted with in dealing with the essentials of the Christian faith. Perhaps it is already clear that on the bases discussed above unity even in the fundamental doctrines appears unattainable. But this is by no means the whole story: the second phrase of the formula we have adopted as schematic reads: in non-essentials liberty. But what are the non-essentials? The variety of opinions on this matter is even more bewildering than those prevailing in the realm of dogmas. As I have already

[14] Waddams, ed., *op. cit.*, p. 52.

indicated, the Eastern Orthodox have adopted the practice of formulating such beliefs in generally acknowledged creeds, catechisms, or fairly homogeneous tradition adhered to by the hierarchy of the autonomous bodies composing the Eastern Orthodox federation. It is this body of dogmas and patristic *theologumena* which binds the otherwise organizationally autonomous constituent bodies and makes them "Orthodox," that is, "right-believing." Moreover, the purity of doctrine, as their name itself indicates, is highly prized and jealously guarded and defended by them. The Orthodox East prides itself on having preserved the purity of Christian faith more completely and faithfully than any other body in Christendom. Thus despite the theoretical distinction between dogmas and *theologumena,* in reality no essential distinction exists between them. At the Evanston meeting in 1954 the Orthodox delegates clearly stated their repudiation of any distinction between the essential and non-essential doctrines by the ringing declaration:

> It is compelling that all doctrines as formulated by the Ecumenical Councils, as well as the totality of the teaching of the Early, Undivided Church, should be accepted. . . . From the Orthodox viewpoint reunion of Christendom with which the World Council of Churches is concerned can be achieved solely on the basis of the total dogmatic Faith of the Early, Undivided Church without either subtraction or alteration. We cannot accept a rigid distinction between essential and non-essential doctrines, and there is no room for comprehensiveness in the Faith. On the other hand, the Orthodox Church cannot accept that the Holy Spirit speaks to us only through the Bible. The Holy Spirit abides and witnesses through the totality of the Church's life and experience.[15]

This is surely plain speaking which leaves no doubt as to the all-inclusiveness of the Orthodox demand, that the entire system of doctrinal tradition current among them must form the basis of reunion. But the case is even more difficult among the Roman Catholics, where many of the Orthodox *theologumena* have already been declared dogmas, and where some, which the latter repudiate, have been added. Pope Pius XI in his encyclical *Mortal-*

[15] *St. Vladimir's Seminary Quarterly* (Fall, 1954–Winter 1955), pp. 19–20.

ium animos made a short shrift of the whole distinction by declaring:

> It is never lawful to employ in connection with articles of faith the distinction invented by some between "fundamental" and "non-fundamental" articles, the former to be accepted by all, the latter being left to the free acceptance of the faithful. The supernatural virtue of faith has as its formal motive the authority of God revealing, and this allows of no such distinction. All true followers of Christ, therefore, will believe the dogma of the Immaculate Conception of the Mother of God with the same faith as they believe the mystery of the august Trinity, the infallibility of the Roman Pontiff in the sense defined by the Oecumenical Vatican Council with the same faith as they believe the Incarnation of our Lord.[16]

Accordingly, all that is contained in the Tridentine Catechism is to all intents and purposes authoritative and binding upon the believers.

Any extended treatment of these doctrines, which Protestants regard as less essential, is not possible; yet we cannot omit a limited notice of some of them. The veneration of saints, and particularly of the Virgin, certainly offers a stumbling block to a *rapprochement* between these communions. Catholics hold that saints are those exemplary Christians who have not only completely fulfilled all that God demanded of them by way of duties, but who have also earned a surplus merit by observing the evangelical counsels besides. Their merits, along with the infinite merit of Christ, form the so-called "treasury of merits" from which the Church, controlling this treasury, dispenses what is needed by those of her members who have come short of the requirements. Thus although the saints cannot save us, they may help us not only by means of their merits but also by their intercessions before the throne of God. This teaching then amply justifies, in fact necessitates, prayers to saints so prevalent and popular among Catholics. But the Church strenuously contends that this is not *worship* of saints—worship belongs only to God—but only *veneration*. I doubt that many

[16] Marchant, *op. cit.*, p. 22.

believers, unskilled in precise theological distinctions, are capable of drawing the fine line between the two concepts.

The case of the veneration of the Virgin Mary is incomparably more complicated: for although she, being only human, holds in reality only the highest rank among the saints, the piety of the ages, particularly of the last hundred years, has elevated her almost to the rank of the co-redemptrix along with her divine Son. The astonishing development of her superveneration (*hyperdoulia*) derives solely from the fact that she bore our Lord Jesus Christ. Starting with practically no theological notion of her exalted rank, by 431 the slippery term *Theotokos,* incautiously interpreted as the Mother of God rather than as the Bearer of God, was already officially introduced. In the Middle Ages the cult of the Virgin reached a high point. But it was Pope Pius IX who began the period of her rapid dogmatic exaltation by publishing, in 1854, the dogma of the Immaculate Conception. This dogma, previously already generally accepted, became even more popular by the alleged appearance of Mary as the Immaculate Conception to the subnormal Bernadette at Lourdes (1858), and more recently her appearance to some children at Fátima, in Portugal. Leo XIII and Pius XII have urged prayers to Mary. Finally, in 1950, Pius XII proclaimed the dogma of Mary's bodily assumption into heaven, whereby she was placed at the right hand of her divine Son, who in turn occupies the place at the right hand of God the Father. Mary is now held to have been entirely sinless. It is impossible, declares the encyclical of Pius XII, that her divine Son "should not honor His beloved mother second only to His Divine Father." The same pope has "dedicated all mankind to her immaculate heart," thus making her the spiritual mother of all believers. Moreover, as no one comes to the Father but through the Son, no one comes to the Son except through His mother. And, finally, the stage is already set for proclaiming her dogmatically as sharing in the redemption accomplished by Christ. All this dizzy exaltation of Mary does not make her the fourth member of the Godhead; but it certainly comes close to it. It is this situation with which the ecumenicists, still thinking of including the

Catholics within the quest for Church unity, must deal. I wonder what they could possibly propose that would be acceptable to both sides and thus bring the divided Christendom together again.

A similar insistence upon the veneration of the saints and the Virgin is expressed by a prominent Russian Orthodox theologian, who writes:

> Perhaps in no other respect does the Ecumenical Movement prove to be so dominated by Protestant thought and interests as in this unconcern for the veneration of Our Lady, so precious and essential to the whole Catholic world. Fr. Sergius Bulgakov . . . pointed out that without unity on this question there can be no unity of faith. And further the same author writes that the problem of veneration of ikons, has never been so much as raised in the Ecumenical Movement. And yet . . . it is one of the most important truths of Christian dogmas. . . . To pass it over in silence and to imagine that it has no real importance for the problem of unity of faith is a great mistake.[17]

Among the Protestants, we must bear in mind, there also exist definite theological traditions, such as the Lutheran, Calvinist, Anglican, Anabaptist, and Methodist. These communions have formulated their theological tenets in creeds and catechisms without any formal distinction between dogmas and doctrines. Nevertheless, such distinction is not denied in principle, and could perhaps be established in fact. It seems to me that the differences among the various theological traditions are not insurmountable, although in some instances quite formidable, and hitherto sufficiently real to keep the denominations apart. Would the Calvinist predestinarians of whatever school be willing to come to terms with their Arminian friends? Would those who are convinced of the rightfulness of the believers' baptism be willing to come to some kind of agreement with the pedobaptist believers? Would the Lutherans, Zwinglians, and the Calvinists arrive at some common understanding in regard to the Lord's Supper? All these and many other examples of theological disagreements among Protestants are so well known

[17] Zander, *op. cit.,* pp. 142–143, 146.

that I do not wish to dwell on them needlessly. But let me add before leaving the subject that I do not hold with those who make light of these differences or even denounce them as if they were not only non-essential, but positively petty, unjustified, and altogether unjustifiable. Such supercilious, censorious, and condemnatory attitudes may only reveal religious indifference on the part of those who show it. There indeed *are* non-essential differences among us—the result of some past or present theological prima donna's self-assertion or of sheer historically fortuitous origin not consciously intended by anyone in particular. All our differences, essential and non-essential, must be humbly submitted to the test of Christ's spirit: but even so, honestly conceived and held convictions will remain and conflict with equally honest beliefs of others. Such differences are inseparable from the exercise of religious freedom; for whereever there is liberty there will inevitably be varieties of opinion. To be ready to surrender all or any of our convictions without a conscientious persuasion as to the new and larger truth only proves that we had no honest conviction in the first place. And let us be reminded that insincere professions for the sake of peace or union may be mere opportunisms or worse—a pious fraud. Even the most desirable ends are never served or justified by wrong means.

But we must not imagine or assume that the so-called noncreedal denominations are without deep-seated theological convictions. Just because the Congregationalists, Baptists, Disciples, or Friends profess no binding creeds, it does not follow that "they do not believe anything," as I have heard it expressed by some very ill-informed people on many an occasion. For that matter, the Baptists and the Disciples are among the most "firm" believers anywhere! I need not remind my readers without coming close to insulting them that the only freedom that these churches claim is to formulate their conscientious beliefs in their own terms—not freedom to repudiate the faith of the historic Christian Church itself! They will find no difficulty, I believe, in accepting the Scriptures as the norm of all faith and morals —since that is their own basic article of faith now. But it will be more difficult for them to accept the historic creeds—the Apostles', the Nicene, or the Chalcedonian—not particularly because they reject the truths enshrined in them, but just because they are binding creeds. As an illustration I may cite the attitude of W. E. Garrison, a leading Disciple, who would reduce the doctrinal basis of Christianity to a simple pledge of loyalty comprised in the phrase "Jesus is Lord." [18] Not that he would not allow any sort of theological elaboration of the phrase; but none could be required as a test for membership or for the ministry.

As for private theological opinions, they flourish like daisies among Protestants, particularly those of the "noncreedal" variety! They are indeed sometimes of the most astonishing kind, and are the principal breeders of splinter groups and what is popularly known as "sects," although I do not know what precise distinction is to be drawn between "sects" and "denominations," unless it be in this realm of "private" theological opinion. Such free views have always existed, and unless we contemplate in connection with the united Church a Holy Office of the Inquisition more effective than the medieval one, they will continue. So long as no one is forced to believe them, perhaps they need not unduly disturb us. We need not complicate the already complicated problem by seriously concerning ourselves with this sort of difficulty.

An attempt to produce ecumenical theology has already been made in a tentative and exploratory way. This shows that the task is being taken seriously. One such work is Walter M. Horton's *Christian Theology: An Ecumenical Approach.*[19] It does not follow the pattern I suggested above and makes no distinction between dogmas and doctrines. But it is useful in establishing areas of fairly general theological agreement or disagreement and thus points out what yet needs to be done. But the author —a "maximalist" by his own confession—seems to ignore the insuperable difficulties of which he must be aware, and thus

[18] W. E. Garrison, *The Quest and Character of a United Church,* p. 225.

[19] Walter M. Horton, *Christian Theology: An Ecumenical Approach* (New York, Harper & Brothers, 1955).

minimizes the task and contributes to the unrealistic attitude generally prevalent among the ecumenicists.

Perhaps this will suffice to suggest the serious nature of the theological reconstruction necessary to integrate the various current theological systems of the existing denominations into an ecumenical synthesis. The undertaking is truly colossal and of breath-taking magnitude, presenting at present insurmountable difficulties. I am frank to confess that for the present and the foreseeable future an attempt to produce a truly integrated ecumenical theology—such as would comprise the Roman Catholic, Eastern Orthodox, and the Protestant traditions and would be acceptable to all of them—appears to me to exceed the bounds of possibility. But I would not, on the other hand, assert dogmatically that the goal will never be reached. For that reason it would seem a rash folly to speak confidently of the shape of things to come as far as the ultimate goal is concerned. At best we may speak of the general direction in which the venture of faith tends. Thus the ecumenical movement, viewed from the point of that which is possible in the present circumstances, reduces itself at most to Pan-Protestantism, although less than that is more likely of attainment. But even that would be a tremendous achievement worthy of our best endeavor.

However, I know that the hardy breed of ecumenicists is far from willing to modify its grandiose dream. To such I address myself in these concluding remarks and bid them consider the cost of a complete theological synthesis, even if for argument's sake we assume that such a thing is possible. From what has already been said it is abundantly evident that the Protestant churches in general and the noncreedal churches in particular would principally pay the cost. For if unity of faith expressed in a theological synthesis is a necessary presupposition of the unity of Christendom—and it seems, for weal or woe, that it is—then a generally accepted creedal statement is a *sine qua non* of such a unity. This is the judgment of W. E. Garrison, who writes: "We cannot avoid the impression that the most influential and articulate leaders of the ecumenical movement are proceeding on the assumption that the attainment of a united Church waits upon the achievement of general theological agreement, though this is often called 'unity on the truth.' "[20] Moreover, since the Roman Catholics and Eastern Orthodox possess an overwhelming numerical preponderance, it does not require too much imagination or a gift of prophecy to realize —indeed to assert—that the only creedal statement acceptable to all would be very close to that held by the majority. Thus Protestantism, and particularly liberal Protestantism, would pay the heaviest price for the coming Great Church.

Nor is it to be confidently assumed that the Protestant hegemony of the World Council of Churches would necessarily continue; in fact, that organization itself would cease to exist as having fulfilled its provisional purpose. Thus unless we should expect that by some miracle the Roman Catholic and Eastern Orthodox churches would be converted to Protestantism—a miracle which I neither anticipate nor can persuade myself to believe in—then the ecumenical Church by sheer numbers and the staunch loyalty to the Catholic traditions would be predominantly Catholic. I am surprised that the papacy has as yet not perceived this inevitable result which its cooperation with the ecumenical movement would lead to, and has not infiltrated it and thus molded it in its own image. Furthermore, I surmise that the inclusion of the Russian Orthodox Church, which is being considered, is inspired by the same motive, and would tend in the same direction.

Such then is likely to be the cost of the theological synthesis necessary to effect the unity of Christendom. Perhaps the proponents of this all-inclusive ecumenical ideal actually think that the goal is worth the cost; but so far I have not seen it explicitly so stated in the pertinent literature. The greater likelihood is that in the flush of their ardent enthusiasm they failed to count the cost in a realistic and critical fashion. For myself, even though I gladly grant the very great values inherent in the movement, I am not ready to seek that unity at any and all costs. I believe that it would be possible to sacrifice too many other

[20] Garrison, *op. cit.*, p. 213.

and real religious values in order to get it. I am not willing to surrender the real gains of the Protestant Reformation, particularly religious freedom. And I fear that by reaching for the ecumenical moon we may well lose what might otherwise be within our grasp.

CHAPTER III

THE PROBLEM OF "ECUMENICAL" POLITY

In the previous chapter we have considered the problems raised by the conflicting concepts of the Church. So far we have left out of consideration the remaining aspects of ecclesiology which are usually treated under the heading of the organization of the Church or of polity. This category includes the definition of valid ministry, the sacraments, as well as the polities proper —namely, the three historic forms of Church order, Congregational, Presbyterian, and Episcopal. For some communions—the Roman Catholic, the Eastern Orthodox, and the Episcopal—the distinction between faith and order hardly exists: orders are as much part and parcel of the dogmatic system as the articles of faith themselves. For most Protestants, however, polity is of secondary significance, that is, non-essential to the substance of faith. Some still derive for it a certain degree of Scriptural sanction; but to others it is the preferred or traditional way of conducting the work of the Church with efficiency and order. Nevertheless, this does not mean that polity is not important; in fact, polities have traditionally been among the principal sources of friction and separation, and as such must be treated as meriting serious attention and accorded proper recognition.

Surely there can be no united Church without a ministry universally recognized as valid. Assuming this obvious truth, the matter becomes as important as the unity in faith which we have discussed previously. The Roman Catholics, the Eastern Orthodox, and most Anglicans and Episcopalians agree that there can be no valid ministry without episcopal ordination by bishops in apostolic succession. The only difference between the first-named and the other two is that submission to the pope is not recognized as the *sine qua non* for the validity of the latters' episcopal orders. In all three communions the bishops are recognized as successors of the apostles, who received their "consecration" directly from the Lord when He breathed on them and thus endowed them with the Holy Spirit. This "grace" has then been passed on in an uninterrupted succession through the centuries by the laying on of hands; and the ordination of priests by bishops in apostolic succession is absolutely essential for the validity of their functions. No other ministry is regarded as valid nor can it be recognized as such in either the present or any future Church. Since the sacraments do not merely convey but effect grace, and their validity depends upon the proper ordination and intention of the priest who administers them, it is obvious that the matter of ordination is of supreme importance.

For the Roman Catholics, the pope is the indispensable and absolutely essential fountainhead of the ordaining grace. For he is the successor of Peter, the Prince of the Apostles, and as such is the Vicar of Christ on earth. Accordingly, even though they recognize the Eastern Orthodox and some others as possessing hierarchy in apostolic succession, yet since the latter are not in communion with the pope, they are regarded as schismatical. Furthermore, those who receive valid ordination at the hands of a Roman Catholic bishop are set apart by reason of their indelible ordination from the rest of the Church. The Tridentine Catechism speaks of them in extravagant terms:

> Bishops and priests being, as they are, God's interpreters and ambassadors, empowered in His name to teach mankind the divine law and the rules of conduct, and holding, as they do, His place on earth, it is evident that no nobler function than theirs can be imagined. Justly,

therefore, are they called not only Angels, but even gods, because of the fact that they exercise in our midst the power and prerogatives of the immortal God.[1]

This, of course, refers primarily to the power of transubstantiating the bread and wine of the sacrament of the altar into the body and blood of our Lord. In words which sound almost blasphemous to Protestant ears, this idea is stated in the Tridentine Catechism as follows:

For the power of consecrating and offering the body and blood of our Lord and of forgiving sins, which has been conferred on them, not only has nothing equal or like to it on earth, but even surpasses human reason and understanding.[2]

This statement is repeated in the pastoral letter sent by the Cardinal of Salzburg (1905) to his diocese:

Where in heaven or on earth is there power like that which a Catholic priest possesses? Mary gave birth to the divine child for this earth but once, but look, the priest does this not once, but hundreds and thousands of times, as often as he celebrates the mass.[3]

Clerical pretensions could hardly go further and higher than that!

Besides, the pope is the living, infallible teaching authority in dogmatic definition of faith and morals. Since the Church has for long recognized two canons of the Christian faith—Scripture and tradition—the pope is the living tradition and the supreme interpreter of Scripture. Even if one were to accept every article of the Catholic faith, but not the dogma of papal infallibility, he would not be a member of the one true Church, but at best a schismatic, as the Eastern Orthodox are declared to be. Aside from the pope, there is no true Church, hierarchy, or priest-

[1] *Catechism of the Council of Trent, for Parish Priests,* tr. John A. McHugh and Charles F. Callan (New York, Joseph F. Wagner, Inc., 1923), p. 318. Used by permission.

[2] *Ibid.*

[3] Quoted in Skydsgaard, *One in Christ,* p. 167.

hood. Consequently, the Roman Catholic Church consists properly only of those possessing sacerdotal powers from the pope—the bishops and the clergy. Lay members depend on the priestly order for valid sacraments through which salvation is mediated to them. It is in this sense that *"extra ecclesiam nulla salus."* This hoary assertion that outside the Roman Church there is no salvation, is reiterated in "The Syllabus of Errors" (1864) in which the pope specifically declares that in Protestantism it is not "possible to be equally pleasing to God as in the Catholic Church." He asserts that it is not feasible to "entertain at least a well-founded hope for the eternal salvation of all those who are in no manner in the true Church of Christ." [4] To this he adds that although

> those who are affected by invincible ignorance about our most holy religion, and who are willing to observe the natural law written into the hearts of all men by God and to obey God . . . in His supreme goodness and pity [God] never would allow . . . to be punished with eternal punishment who did not voluntarily commit a sin. But it is known that Catholic dogma states that nobody outside of the Catholic Church can be saved and those who defy the authority of the Church and its definitions and are divided from the unity of the Church and the successor of Peter, the Roman pontiff . . . cannot gain eternal life.[5]

Recently, this pronouncement was used—with a curious perversion of its meaning, it seems to me—to silence Father Leonard Feeney in Boston when he told his Protestant audiences that they cannot be saved except in the Roman Church.

Moreover, the pope is in his own person the supreme ruler not only of the Roman Church but of the entire Christendom. Not only does he possess jurisdiction over "heretics and schismatics," as the Tridentine Catechism asserts, [6] but every baptized Christian, no matter to what communion he belongs, is claimed

[4] "Syllabus of Errors," in Philip Schaff, *The Creeds of Christendom* (New York, 1877), II, 217–218.

[5] Anne Fremantle, ed., *The Papal Encyclicals in Their Historical Context* (New York: G. P. Putnam's Sons & Coward-McCann, Inc., 1956), pp. 131–132. Used by permission.

[6] *Catechism,* p. 101.

as a subject to his authority, whether he acknowledges it or not. This is the assertion made by Pope Pius IX in his letter to Kaiser Wilhelm I during the *Kulturkampf*.[7]

Passing now to a consideration of the position of the Eastern Orthodox, we find them to differ from the Roman Catholic doctrine principally in the matter of the papal infallibility and supremacy. They define the Church as "the community of the faithful united by faith, hierarchy and sacraments." Thus they stress the importance of the episcopacy in apostolic succession as strongly as the Roman Catholics. The clergy depend for valid ordination, and therefore for sacerdotal powers, upon their bishops:

"The Episcopal succession from the Apostles," asserted the Orthodox delegation at Evanston,

> constitutes an historic reality in the life and structure of the Church and one of the presuppositions of her unity through the ages. . . . Thus when we are considering the problem of Church unity we cannot envisage it in any other way than as the complete restoration of the total faith and the total Episcopal Structure of the Church which is basic to the sacramental life of the Church. We would not pass judgment upon those of the separated communions. However, it is our conviction that in these communions certain basic elements are lacking which constitute the reality of the fulness of the Church. We believe that the return of the communions to the Faith of the ancient, united, and indivisible Church of the Seven Ecumenical Councils . . . shall alone produce the desired reunion of all separated Christians. For only the unity and fellowship of Christians in a common Faith shall have as a necessary result their fellowship in the sacraments and their indissoluble unity in love, as members of one and the same Body of one Church of Christ.[8]

Failing these demands, the Orthodox delegation declared, "the whole approach to the problem of reunion is entirely unacceptable from the standpoint of the Orthodox Church." Or, to quote a distinguished Orthodox theologian's opinion:

[7] Skydsgaard, *op. cit.*, p. 84.

[8] "Declaration of the Orthodox Delegates" in *St. Vladimir's Seminary Quarterly* (Fall, 1954–Winter, 1955), p. 20.

Apostolic succession is its [unity's] necessary condition, but in itself is insufficient for recognizing its bearer as a bishop in the Orthodox or Catholic meaning of the term. The Episcopate is essentially a eucharistic institution. A bishop is, in the first instance, one who celebrates the sacrament of the eucharist . . . to the faithful who, through the sacrament become the Body of Christ—the Church.[9]

The intransigent stand of these two communions as to the absolute necessity of ordination in the apostolic succession for the valid priesthood is now, I hope, sufficiently demonstrated. The second proposal to be considered by us is that of the historic episcopate. All Anglicans and American Protestant Episcopalians demand that the historic episcopate find acceptance, and be assigned its proper function, in the new Church of the future. For the majority among them this necessarily implies episcopacy in apostolic succession. Yet there are exceptions; thus Canon Wedel of the Washington Cathedral, although he doubts that "any solution of the problem of Church unity is really possible except under episcopal church order," [10] yet he would be satisfied with the historic episcopate without apostolic succession. He writes bluntly:

But unless a view of episcopal Church order can extricate itself from this Roman dogma of a vicarial Apostolic succession and priesthood, its rejection by evangelical Christendom is foreordained. This theory of the ministry a Biblical Protestantism will never accept. The doctrine of Apostolic Succession as a vicarial ministry must go.[11]

He defines the historic episcopacy as "a functional organ of the Body of Christ in time and space." I doubt whether he means what the Methodists mean by their episcopacy; nevertheless, it comes close to it. Unfortunately, powerful sections of world Anglicanism, and the American Church Union of the Episcopal Church, look with abhorrence upon Canon Wedel's theories and repudiate them in the strongest terms.

[9] Zander, *Vision and Action,* p. 168.
[10] T. O. Wedel, *The Coming Great Church,* p. 133.
[11] *Ibid.,* pp. 146, 154.

In the third place, the demand for the episcopal order finds expression in the so-called "functional" episcopacy, such as has been instituted in the Methodist churches. Lutheran bodies on the Continent have been increasingly turning to this form of superintendency, for they have had a similar form of oversight and centralized organization from the beginning of their existence. For that matter, the Lutheran Church of Sweden has actually preserved its episcopal order in apostolic succession. Calvin likewise had no objection to bishops of this kind, and some Calvinist churches have retained the episcopal office, as for instance the Reformed Church of Hungary or the Czech Brethren Evangelical Church (which, however, calls the head of the Church "Synodical Senior"). Nevertheless, this form of episcopacy, which makes no pretension to apostolic succession or even to historic episcopacy, is not recognized by the Catholic communions. But then the vast bulk of the latter do not recognize the Anglican orders either!

Protestant churches generally either possess functional episcopacy, of which I have just spoken, or no episcopacy at all, unless one wishes to revive the Reformation claim that a presbyter and a bishop originally represented the same order, although not the same function. Accordingly, their ministry is ordained either congregationally or presbyterially; and unless this kind of ordination is recognized as valid by the Episcopal or Catholic churches, the chances of unity in the coming Church are negligible.

The same impasse exists in regard to the sacraments. According to the Roman Catholic teaching, the sacraments do not merely symbolize grace; they impart grace. That is what is meant by the phrase *ex opere operato,* that is, by virtue inherent in themselves. A sacrament is valid when it is correctly ministered or performed. The Church claims that this secures the act against subjective conditions on the part of the recipient which might render it uncertain. But if this were the whole definition, the sacraments would appear to partake of the character of magic. Therefore, the Church guards itself against such a charge by insisting that the recipient must be in the state of grace, partaking of the sacrament "sacramentally and spiritually," for otherwise the grace inherent in it would "be of no avail to a soul which lives not by the spirit."[12] In other words, although the sacrament is valid in itself, it is not effective unless the recipient does his share. This applies to all sacraments with the exception of infant baptism. But does not this reservation nullify the force of the *ex opere operato* concept?

Furthermore, although I do not deem it necessary to deal extensively with all seven sacraments, yet for a closer understanding of the gulf fixed between the Protestant and the Catholic apprehension of the subject we cannot pass over at least the sacrament of the altar. There the difference between the two concepts bulks fully as large as in the teaching regarding the sacrament of the Holy Orders, with which we have already dealt. The dogma of transubstantiation adopted by the Lateran Council of 1215 asserts that in the act of transubstantiation the accidents of the elements, bread and wine, remain the same while their substance changes into the body and blood of our Lord. This concept has remained essentially unchanged ever since. *The Canons and Decrees of the Council of Trent* declare that "In the Eucharist are contained truly, really, and substantially, the body and blood, together with the soul and divinity of our Lord Jesus Christ, and consequently the whole Christ." Furthermore, "The whole Christ is contained under each species, and under every part of each species, when separated." It is not necessary for the lay communicant to partake of both elements in order to partake of "the whole Christ." Consequently, he receives only the bread. In further defining the significance of the mass, it is said to be, first of all, the perpetual sacrifice of Christ upon the cross, in which He offers Himself daily on the thousands of Catholic altars for the atonement of sins of both the living and the dead. For many masses are said for the benefit of souls in purgatory. But besides being a sacrifice, it is also a sacrament. As such the consecrated bread, either while the mass is being performed or when it is "reserved," becomes an object of worship. And finally, as has already been

[12] *Catechism*, p. 243.

mentioned, it may serve as the sacrament of holy communion, wherein it becomes the spiritual food whereby the soul is nurtured and built into the mystical Body of Christ.

We may mention in passing that besides the seven sacraments, the Catholic churches also recognize the so-called sacramentals —such as rosaries, crucifixes, pictures and medals of saints and particularly of the Virgin, holy water, and other pious objects and devices. The piety of the ordinary Catholic believer is commonly more concerned with these paraphernalia than with the essentials.

As for the Orthodox, they agree with the Roman Catholics that there are seven sacraments. It makes no difference that all are not specifically mentioned in the Scriptures; nor is it permissible to make a distinction between the two actually instituted by the Lord and the other five. As for the Eucharist, I cite the Russian *Catechism* of Metropolitan Philaret which represents the commonly accepted teaching of all Eastern Orthodox. Liturgy, which is the term used for the Eucharist, is there defined as "the mystery wherein the believer, under the appearance of bread and wine, eats the very Body and Blood of Christ toward eternal life." There is no essential difference between the Roman Catholic and Orthodox concepts of the change occurring in the eucharistic elements, although the latter attempts no explanation of the mystery. Philaret's *Catechism* simply states that in the sacred act "the bread and wine transform or transubstantiate themselves (*prelagayutsya ili presushchestvlyayutsya*) into the true Body of Christ and the true Blood of Christ." "The word transubstantiation (*presushchestvlenie*) does not connote the manner in which the bread and wine transform themselves into the Body and Blood of the Lord, for that is not comprehended by anyone but God alone." The effect of the communion—which by the way, is ministered in both kinds, the bread being soaked in the wine—is "the closer union with Jesus Christ Himself and participation through Him in eternal life." [13]

It is of interest in this connection to note that at the recent

[13] Metropolitan Philaret, *Prostranny Khristiansky Katekhisis* (Berlin, n.d.), pp. 66, 69, 70.

Anglo-Russian Theological Conference the Anglican delegation asserted that although the XXXIX Articles make a distinction between the two Dominican and the other five sacraments, "In the liturgical practice of the Church of England Confirmation, Penance, Holy Orders, Matrimony, and Unction are clearly treated as Sacraments. The Book of Common Prayer provides forms for administering the first four of these, and the Convocation of Canterbury in 1935 approved a form for the administration of Unction. In the forms of administration the sacramental principle is maintained." [14]

Without discussing the obviously grave and, in my judgment, insurmountable difference between the Catholic and Protestant concepts of the sacraments, it seems more to the point to discuss the different views of baptism and the Lord's Supper extant among Protestants. In the first place, the principal difference about baptism concerns those denominations which adhere to infant or to believers' baptism. The Reformers—Lutheran, Calvinist, and Anglican—have retained infant baptism on grounds not altogether faultless. For Luther it was a mode of baptismal regeneration; for Calvin, it was several things, but principally the New Testament form of the circumcision of the Old; for both it symbolized that the child belongs to the family of God gathered in the Church. But they were likewise conscious that one basically important element, namely, the confession of faith on the part of the baptized infant, has been lacking. Accordingly, when the child baptized in infancy reached the age when it could consciously assume the vows which had been made on its behalf by the parents, it did so in the rite of confirmation, which thus provided what was hitherto lacking.

It was at this point that the Anabaptists and later Baptists differed from the pedobaptists: they insisted that the rite could not be validly administered to anyone except to such as were able to make a profession of their faith prior to baptism. Their difficulty consisted, however, in defining the status of the child prior to baptism: Was he in any way related to the Church? Other subsidiary matters, such as the mode of baptism—immer-

[14] Waddams, ed., *Anglo-Russian Theological Conference,* p. 102.

sion or sprinkling—need not detain us, since they are not generally held to be of the essence of the sacrament. But the still outstanding differences between those who practice infant or believers' baptism must be resolved, before unity can be achieved, either by mutual recognition or by some other solution. I would urge, however, that honest conviction in these matters be accorded the respectful consideration which it deserves.

As for the Lord's Supper, the existing differences, although serious, are not, in my judgment, insurmountable. Lutherans insist on a view that the Real Presence exists "in, with and under" the bread and wine, and assert that this presence is not merely spiritual. But they will not go beyond this assertion. Luther proved himself a violent literalist when in his Marburg conference with Zwingli in 1529 he insisted on the literal meaning of our Lord's word: "This is my body." But he rightly refused to regard as wholly satisfactory Zwingli's interpretation of the sacrament as a mere memorial of Christ's death, although it is most likely that the latter subsequently changed his mind on the point. To be sure, this was and is one of the meanings of the sacrament, for our Lord Himself has declared: "Do this in remembrance of me." But it is more than a memorial. It must furthermore be noted that the other great leader of the Lutheran movement, Melanchthon, was always troubled about Luther's formulation of the doctrine of the Lord's Supper and never accepted consubstantiation. At last in 1535 he arrived at his own definition of the "essential in the Eucharist" which to him consisted of a "spiritual communion with Christ," a concept closely approximating Calvin's. When he made this view known to Luther, the latter surprisingly did not attack it; apparently, he was willing to tolerate it in Melanchthon, even though he would not accept it for himself.[15] Calvin emphasized, both against Luther and Zwingli, the spiritual presence of the Lord for the believer who appropriates it by faith; this to him was the essential meaning of the sacrament. He would have had no difficulty in accepting the term "real presence," if it did not

[15] C. L. Manschreck, *Melanchthon, the Quiet Reformer* (New York, Abingdon Press, 1958), p. 235. Used by permission.

necessarily involve the concept of the ubiquity of the glorified body of the Lord. To him the spiritual presence *was* the real presence. Surely, there exists a possibility of a large measure of agreement among the various communions of Protestants on this term "real presence," or at least of mutual tolerance of the diverse views. I am hopeful that in time it may be reached. I rejoice that the Federation of Evangelical Lutheran Churches in India (with the exception of the Missouri Synod), who have been negotiating with the Church of South India, accepted (1955) for their own an agreed-upon formula which asserted that "the Lord's Supper is essentially the mystery of the real personal presence of our Lord Jesus Christ," but that "the manner of Christ's presence in the bread and wine of the sacrament is a mystery which our minds cannot comprehend . . . We believe that as we receive the bread and wine . . . we receive the body and blood of Christ in a spiritual manner. . . ." [16]

In the third place, the concept of the unified Church demands a consideration of the three existing polities—Congregational, Presbyterian, and Episcopal. How are they to be united into one, if that is what the ecumenicists intend to do? Are they to be subordinated one to another or retained essentially unchanged in a free federation of churches? Attempts at a solution of this thorny problem have occasioned considerable conflicts. Again the "Catholic" communions need not concern us, for their church order is part and parcel of their dogmatic systems, and as such no change in its fundamentals is likely. We must pass on to the consideration of this problem within Protestantism, where alone some kind of solution is possible.

One of the most frequently mentioned and tenaciously advocated schemes is that of a return to the New Testament or apostolic pattern, or at most to the period of the "undivided" Church—presumably up to the Photian schism of the ninth century. The Disciples originally repudiated all "denominations" with their "man-made creeds," and denounced all ecclesiastical divisions as "a horrid evil," un-Christian and un-Scriptural. They

[16] *News Sheet of the Church of South India Council in Great Britain,* July, 1955, p. 2.

advocated a return to the plain teachings of the New Testament. Their watchword was, "Where the Scriptures speak, we speak; where the Scriptures are silent, we are silent." And although this emphasis on church unity has remained a matter of deep and abiding concern with them to this day, yet their strongly emphasized theological tenets and sacramental practices render them a denomination among other denominations. It may also be worth while to point out that what they professed to find in the Bible was conditioned by the time in which they lived—they did not escape historical influences which they pretended to have leapfrogged! Moreover, their advocacy of the return to the conditions of the primitive Church makes them representatives of a much larger company among various denominations proposing restorationism as the pattern of the unified Church. It must, however, be pointed out that at present such outstanding Disciples as Morrison and Garrison decisively repudiate the traditional "restorationist" doctrine of their fellowship.

But the modern critical study of the New Testament discloses a variety of organizational patterns and of doctrinal differences in the early Church. The first century organization was originally charismatic, "not vested in any formally named or ordained class but belonging automatically to those who were actually doing the greater part of the work of the Church," as John Knox reminds us.[17] He interprets the term "bishops" and "deacons" in Philippians 1:1 as referring "perhaps to the core of workers in the Philippian church who were rulers ('bishops') because they were also servants ('deacons')."[18] This interpretation would make the early Church approximate what is now known as the Congregational polity, although with essential differences. But an over-all authority cannot be altogether ruled out, either: for in Jerusalem the apostles under the leadership of James, the brother of the Lord, exercised authority over the Jewish Christian congregations; while Paul also insisted on being recognized as the spiritual father of the churches he himself

[17] John Knox, *The Early Church and the Coming Great Church* (New York, Abingdon Press, 1955), p. 91. Used by permission.

[18] *Ibid.*, p. 92.

had founded, as is shown in the case of the churches in Corinth and particularly in Galatia. Thus a faint trace of the Episcopal polity is likewise distinguishable.

Moreover, there existed dissensions and disputes within these Christian congregations: there were conflicts between the Jewish and the Greek Christians and between Paul's converts and Judaizers. Paul bitterly denounced the incipient repudiation of his apostleship by the churches of Galatia and Corinth; and he likewise condemned the various sectarian parties among the Corinthians; and he warned the Ephesian elders against the "wolves not sparing the flock" (Acts 20:18–35).

As for the differences in doctrine, these were partly hidden by the fact that the only creedal formula generally accepted was the short confession, "Jesus is Lord and Christ" (Acts 2:36). Otherwise doctrine was not formulated further, and this led to acute differences between Judaizers and Pauline Greek Christians, as we may see in the sharp rebuke administered by Paul to Peter at Antioch. Moreover, as long as the expectation of the speedy second coming of the Lord filled the hearts of Christians with lively hopes, there was no compelling reason for uniformity either in doctrine or in organization. This then obviated all permanent planning for the future—the Church had no future on earth. But when this fervent hope failed of realization, the thinking of the Church gradually underwent a basic readjustment and eventuated in a fundamental reconstruction. Accordingly, it is plain that the first century Church cannot serve as a pattern for the present or the future Church.

The three basic reforms which the Church carried through during the second century comprised, first, a creedal development, based on what was regarded as apostolic tradition. It took the form of the Old Roman Symbol, which by the year 200 was transformed into the Apostles' Creed. Dr. Knox remarks that "the creed . . . cannot be traced earlier than the second century, but the promise of it, and the essential substance of it, can be clearly discerned in the first." [19] In the second place, the reform comprised the New Testament canon, for which, how-

[19] *Ibid.*, p. 119.

ever, the earliest known evidence is to be found only in Irenaeus. Justin Martyr does not know it. The Muratorian fragment (*c.* 200), Tertullian, and Clement of Alexandria bear witness to it. In the third place, the organization of the ancient Catholic Church developed early into the monarchical episcopate. First Clement is our earliest source in which bishops are referred to as "successors to the apostles." And the Letters of Ignatius are, of course, our most extensive testimony to the existence of monarchical bishops in some of the churches, Antioch perhaps the earliest; but the Roman church is not among them. Dr. Knox concludes that "the institution of episcopacy does represent a true and all but inevitable sequel to the apostolic office and function." [20]

Such being the situation in the Christian Church during the first and second centuries, the restitutionists could still find in it valuable suggestions for the pattern of the future Church, but could hardly advocate a return to that primitive condition *in toto*. At least, such a return could not be effected without wholesale and basic revisions, modifications, additions, and other radical changes which would make their proposal not at all preferable to other patterns.

Next in order, one commonly advocated proposal propounds the integration of the best and most valuable features of each separate ecclesiastical communion into the unified future Church. This eclectic theory stresses the supposed possession of particular doctrinal and/or organizational special values, or cherished traditions or characteristics on the part of each denomination: the Anglican or Episcopal churches as possessing the historic episcopate and the Book of Common Prayer; the Lutherans as placing special emphasis on justification by faith alone; the Calvinistic churches as stressing biblical theology, discipline, and the presbyterial system; the Methodists as abounding in evangelistic fervor and bubbling enthusiasm; the Baptists as upholding the tenet of believers' baptism; the Congregationalists as insisting on the autonomy of the local churches and the responsibility of the lay members for the work of the

[20] *Ibid.*, p. 120.

Church; and so forth in relation to every other major denomination. The proposal asserts that since each separate ingredient is good and valuable, combining them all together in one lump, or so to speak homogenizing them, must produce the best possible results. Let us see how this optimistic eclectic method would work.

First of all, let us apply this theory to the three historic polities. We need not speculate or theorize about such a combination, because we have actual examples of it in history and in contemporaneous practice. Suppose that we integrate the Congregational and the Presbyterian polities; the former asserts the radical autonomy of the local congregation exclusive of any outside authority, for even the principle of fellowship with other churches does not necessitate the acceptance of their judgment or opinion by any given local congregation. Associations, conferences, and councils possess only delegated authority and exercise merely advisory functions, since they are regarded as instruments of the churches. Moreover, the Congregational polity is not merely a *modus operandi,* but embodies the Reformation principle of the priesthood of all believers. Without a vigorous assertion and practice of this principle, no Church, whether present or future, can exert its full powers: for it imposes full responsibility for the entire program of the Church upon each individual member, lay and clerical alike. Every member of the Church must be about his Father's business—not delegate it to a paid staff! Such a sense of commitment is essential to every local congregation, no matter what denominational label it bears. From this definition it is clear that I do not mean the sort of Congregationalism which C. C. Morrison condemns as the "essential Protestant heresy." [21] He really has Independency in mind. The Presbyterian polity, on the other hand, places actual authority in the presbyteries, synods, and the General Assembly, to which the local congregations are subordinated. Thus the two polities in these respects are mutually exclusive and cannot be combined in such a way as to leave both completely and fully

[21] C. C. Morrison, *What Is Christianity?* (Chicago, Willett, Clark & Co., 1940), pp. 233–242.

intact. In combining them, if the Presbyterian polity with its authority over the local congregations prevails, obviously the Congregational polity cannot retain its principles and functions to the full. Should the Congregational polity prevail, the Presbyterian would thereby be modified in its most characteristic feature. If neither polity obtains the upper hand, the result would be a polity without the virtues of either of the parent stocks. Thus the most probable outcome of the experiment would be either presbyterianized Congregationalism or congregationalized Presbyterianism. In fact, this kind of polity did flourish in eighteenth century Connecticut, having been introduced in 1708 by the Saybrook Platform and being known occasionally and aptly as Presbygationalism. This is the lesson of history wherever the attempt has been tried, as for instance in the Plan of Union of 1801 between the Presbyterians and the Congregationalists. And the remarkable thing about that experiment is that the Presbyterians repealed it first. If then we add to this amalgam the Episcopal polity with its centralized supreme powers of the bishop (with or without the apostolic succession), with his right of veto capable of overriding the decisions of whatever lower jurisdiction or administrative body—not to say the mere local congregation—might exist, then neither the Presbyterian nor the Congregational polities could retain their undiminished vigor. The strongest polity—the Episcopal—would inevitably secure hegemony, while the two weaker ones would play a very subordinate role.

The same may be said in regard to the integration of worship patterns and usages, in which the liturgical would inevitably replace or modify the nonliturgical. This is in plain evidence at present among most of the churches of nonliturgical tradition. I need not remind you of the radical changes which the chancel has undergone with the separation of the lectern from the pulpit and the placing of the communion table—or what is already commonly called the altar—in the center. The vestment investment of the choir and of the minister has been steadily on the increase; the cassock and the surplice, not to say anything about the stole, are already worn by some choirs, while the minister strives not to be left too far behind. At present, I believe, these practices or "reforms" are still largely a fashion without conscious premeditation of substituting liturgical for nonliturgical worship. But it is quite likely to come of age and reveal explicitly its inherent theological implications. Canon Wedel insists that the future Church must accept the Book of Common Prayer for its general use in worship. Certainly, the trend is already in that direction.

The remarkable feature of this liturgical trend among the Protestants is its contrast with the current Roman Catholic liturgical revival. For the latter, following patterns from the pre-Counterreformation worship, exhibits the opposite tendencies to those characteristic of the Protestant movement. The altar is converted into a communion table and moved into the nave of the church, and the priest stands behind it, facing the congregation. The excessively ornate vestments and rites are simplified, and congregational participation in the worship is encouraged. Accordingly, there is hope that after the lapse of some fifty or more years Protestants might emulate this Catholic liturgical revival and thus restore some of their own practices.

But to return to the question of polities: Is it necessary for unity of Christendom, or at least of Protestantism, that they be integrated? Is it the *sine qua non* of any such proposal? The dominant tendency among the ecumenicists certainly points in that direction, and most of the suggested patterns of the future Church are elaborations of some such eclecticism or integration. But in my view this is neither necessary, essential, nor desirable. Since a polity is not of dogmatic validity or an article of faith, but distinctly of secondary significance, it should be a matter of free choice and subject to Christian liberty. It is important, but not all important. There is no reason why all Christians *must* conduct ecclesiastical concerns in precisely the same manner. Once we have given up the notion that there is some Scriptural precept imposing one or another polity upon the Church universal, we should not try to create a mandatory precept of our own making. We may attain the goal of unified Protestantism in essentials without integrating the polities and by retaining them essentially unchanged, existing peacefully side by side. I intend to elaborate this concept later and therefore do not choose to deal with it extensively in this connection. Suffice it to say that I have in mind the pattern suggested by Bishop Dun in his book on *Prospecting for a United Church.* Like myself, he expresses a doubt whether the diverse polities could be amicably accommodated under a single roof, and suggests: "Perhaps we should dream, rather, in terms of a 'center,' to use a contemporaneous architectural term, a central structure and other structures gathered around it, all forming a unity and with the internal channels of communication wide open." [22] But of that, later.

Summing up our discussion regarding the probable changes the united Church would involve in its organizational order or polities, it again appears quite clear that at present or in the near or foreseeable future no mutually satisfactory or acceptable arrangement is possible between the Catholic and Protestant communions. Their systems are so far apart that any conceivable *rapprochement* would necessarily have to take the form of surrender—and it would not be a surrender of the Catholics to the Protestants, of that I am certain! But unity does not mean uniformity—as has been said times without number but must be said again. In matters of conviction, force fails. History of Christendom teaches one lesson unmistakably—namely, that religious conviction cannot be coerced or generated by outward means. The only rule of the Church is freedom in love which engenders unity in diversity. The Church is freedom limited by love. Hence, the quest for the unity should not involve surrenders, but mutually acceptable adjustments and accommodations. I do not wish to be understood as dogmatically asserting that no such mutual agreements can ever be arrived at. I am speaking only of the present and the foreseeable future.

Accordingly, the problem reduces itself to an accommodation among the Protestant denominations where, despite the many and serious obstacles and barriers, the task does not appear wholly insurmountable. Assuming that a will to greater unity

[22] Angus Dun, *Prospecting for a United Church,* p. 109.

exists and will continue, and that it is generally conceded among them that practical results depend upon delimitation of the objectives to themselves alone and not beyond their borders, the inevitable conclusion forces itself upon us to restrict our quest to this possible and attainable goal. Many of our existing ecclesiastical bodies belong essentially to a given family of churches, such as Lutheran, Presbyterian, Congregational, Episcopal, or Baptist. There exists little, if any, reason why each one of these denominational families should not be united into one comprehensive body. Other subsidiary and in no way essential reasons separate other denominations. The really formidable barriers exist only between the Catholic and Protestant communions. And even there the proposal I am making does not imply that we Protestants are separating ourselves irrevocably and for ever from our Catholic brethren: we recognize that within their churches are those who possess the Spirit of Christ and are therefore members of the mystical Body of Christ. But the barriers which otherwise separate us are so great that they force us either to postpone all efforts of seeking a united Church now and for an indefinite period in the future or to proceed with the more modest but decidedly more realistic aims immediately. It seems that the part of wisdom is to choose the latter alternative.

CHAPTER IV

A REALISTIC APPROACH TO THE QUEST FOR UNITY

It appears reasonably clear from our previous considerations that to aim at ecumenicity in the maximal sense of that word is at present an unattainable ideal, a mirage. In avowing that fact in a plain, bald fashion I feel the same hesitancy in making the statement as do the ecumenical leaders who resort to all manner of circumlocution in order to hint at the same thing. But I believe that the fact has to be realistically faced, fairly and carefully examined, and clearly and unambiguously stated. That is what I aim to do, not as one unaware or unappreciative of the desirability of the ecumenical goal, but as one who, just because he strives to make it effective and productive, chooses the limited possible as against the unlimited impossible. My regrets in this connection are particularly keen as far as the Eastern Orthodox are concerned, for I had hoped that a way might be found to establish a closer understanding with them. But I sympathize with the "agony" through which they are passing, as one of their leaders expressed it recently. Nevertheless, we are evidently forced to consider a limited objective which aims at the unity of some Protestant communions, or at best of all Protestantism, but not at all-inclusive ecumenicity. Thus it seems better to abandon the use of the maximal term as inaccurate and therefore misleading. The term "ecumenical" can never properly mean anything else than "catholic" or "universal," "pertaining to the whole Church," and as such *must* include all communions generally acknowledged as comprising Christendom. If we are forced to leave out of consideration the substance of the term, we must be willing to sacrifice the term as well. I understand that Dr. Visser 't Hooft, realizing the dilemma, occasionally defines the term as denoting "the consciousness of and desire for Christian unity," and many follow him in this usage. Such definition would indeed reduce the scope to the factual, though at present not explicitly acknowledged, limits of the movement, but at the cost of emptying the term of its real and proper connotation. I prefer to use words in the meaning they are intended to convey, rather than impose on them a radically novel connotation. In other words, I prefer to call a spade a spade instead of a bulldozer. For the latter usage must necessarily lead to a sizable misunderstanding.

Nor can those escape the charge of misusing the term who continue to use it in the hope that they are "leaving the door open" for the Catholics to join us Protestants at some future time. For the word must express a present reality, not a mere future possibility. Moreover, the proposal renders its advocates subject to the charge of almost fantastic unreality. For can they make themselves really believe that either the Roman Catholics or the Eastern Orthodox would ever be induced not only to give up their exclusive claims, but be actually willing to accept what we are offering them as the price of joining us? That would place them in the company of Alice in Wonderland who, as is well known, was able to believe as many as six impossible things by practicing the art before breakfast!

We may now turn our attention to a few representative plans for the creation of the future Church. The simplest and readiest for immediate action is the so-called Greenwich Plan. It goes back for its inception to the resolution adopted by the Congregational-Christian Council held at Grinnell, Iowa, in 1946. The latter requested the Federal Council of Churches to call a conference with the view to explore ways to a closer union with other denominations. This appeal found support next year in a similar resolution adopted at the International Convention of the Disciples of Christ. In due time (1949) the conference was held at Greenwich, Connecticut, where official delegates of nine denominations—of which the Methodists, Disciples of Christ, Presbyterians, Congregational-Christians, and Evangelical Reformed were the most numerous—agreed on seeking "an organic union." They constituted themselves into a continuing body under the name of "The Conference on Church Union," and elected Bishop Ivan Lee Holt as their president.

The Drafting Committee drew up a plan which was discussed at a convocation held in Cleveland in 1951, and after further elaboration the final text was adopted at the conference at Greenwich in 1953. The distinctive feature of this plan is that it seeks to bring together "into one body three types of churches which already recognize one another's ministries and sacraments but are accustomed to operate under somewhat different forms of organization"—that is, Congregational, Episcopal, and Presbyterian. This organic union is to be accomplished on the basis of "the Common Faith" of which they declare that in its "essentials . . . we are already one." The "common belief" is not expressed in any of the historic creeds (of which nothing is explicitly affirmed) but in a newly prepared statement. But it is not clear whether the acceptance of this statement would be required as a condition of membership in the United Church of Christ.

First of all, the statement asserts belief in "God the Father; in Jesus Christ, his only Son, our Savior; in the Holy Spirit, our Guide and Comforter." This is intended as an affirmation of the trinitarian doctrine; but if so, then the statement is gravely faulty. Taken as it stands, without reading anything into it, it is really tritheistic, not trinitarian. It asserts belief in three gods, not one God in three of His divine revelations, as the historic Niceno-Constantinopolitan Creed defines it—one *ousia* in three *hypostases*. One would have supposed that the Congregationalists, who had suffered a grievous Unitarian schism some century and a half ago on account of similar looseness of language in stating the trinitarian doctrine, would have known better than to repeat the mistake; and that all who are aware of the violent rejection of Christianity by the Muslims on this very ground would likewise have avoided giving even an appearance of evil. Nevertheless, the framers of the Greenwich Plan once again committed the serious blunder.

Furthermore, one may also notice that the phrase used in regard to our Lord designates Him merely as "his only Son, our Savior." Even the formula adopted by the World Council of Churches goes further and stipulates faith in Jesus Christ "as God and Saviour." I do not suppose that any evasion of the more explicit statement was intended, but that to the framers of the statement the phrase was equivalent to the assertion of our Lord's divinity. And yet, anyone who is even superficially acquainted with the Arian controversy knows that the phrase "son of God" was Arius' favorite expression, and that he interpreted it in a sense which denied both our Lord's divinity and humanity. To Arius, Jesus Christ was neither God nor man. Would it not be safer, in order to avoid any possibility of plunging the Church once more into the long-drawn-out struggle over the matter—particularly with the International Association of Evangelicals—to use the explicit language which is not subject to this kind of misuse? I repeat once more that I do not for a moment believe that the proponents had any intention other than to assert the substance of the Nicene Creed. For in specifying the condition of membership in the local churches, they say that the prospective members are received "on profession of faith in Jesus Christ as divine Lord and Savior." But why did they allow the discrepancy between the two statements cited? Furthermore, nothing is said about the Incarnation and the two natures. Why not use language which precludes any doubt about the matter and which clearly says what the proponents mean?

The statement of the "common faith" then goes on to include the belief in the Holy Catholic Church, the Scriptures of the Old and New Testaments, the forgiveness of sins, and the life everlasting. It then asserts the obligation of the Church's unity, although it recognizes "diversity of gifts, concerns, and ministrations," and assures all of "freedom in ways of worship and of witness." The statement concludes with a dedication of the United Church to "the furtherance of the Lord's redemptive work in the world."

It would have been better, had a more comprehensive statement regarding the "common faith" been agreed upon by the representatives of denominations that, as a matter of fact, individually and collectively profess a far more explicit set of doctrines. This statement is obviously inadequate to satisfy even the minimum requirements of such communions as the Protestant Episcopal and the Lutheran. Does it really satisfy the Presbyterians, the Methodists, the Evangelical Reformed, or for that matter the Congregational Christians?

In the second place, we come to the plan proposing an integration of the three polities into one. The local church is described in terms presumably meant to represent the historic Congregational polity. "The United Church of Christ recognizes and respects the freedom of each local church in the discharge of its local responsibilities, and it also provides for an orderly exercise of the mutual responsibilities of the local churches in relation to their sister churches in the United Church. The local church brings into the United Church of Christ, without essential change, all the present structure and procedure." But is it really Congregational "without essential change"? The two historic principles of that polity have ever been the autonomy of the local church and the voluntary fellowship with other churches, without any acknowledgment of authority on the part of the latter. Since the polity of the United Church provides for an authoritative presbytery which has the right to examine and install all ministers of the United Church, plus the episcopal supervision at the highest level, it is clear that an essential change in Congregational polity *is* proposed. I have noticed that it has become fairly common to equate the Congregational polity with nothing more than the responsibility of a local congregation for its local needs. The other basic principle, the nonrecognition of any authority over the local congregation, is quietly ignored, as is evident in the Greenwich Plan. I deny that no "essential change" is contemplated, or that the Congregational polity as integrated by the plan would function in its "present structure and procedure."

The Presbyterian polity is integrated into the structure at the level at which it now operates; namely, in presbyteries in which all ministers would hold their membership and which would have the exclusive right to examine and ordain candidates for the ministry, although this would be done on the recommendation of the local church. The presbytery would likewise install the minister in his charge at the request and with the participation of the local church. I can discern no essential change in the present functions of the presbyteries save as they would be affected by the episcopal structure above them.

As for the Episcopal polity, it is defined in terms of the Methodist concept of the office, that is, as the administrative superintendency. The bishop participates in and presides at all ordinations, and without his approval ministers cannot change from one denominational category to another. His relation to the three categories of membership is described as that of an adviser to the Congregational, an executive in the Presbyterian, and an administrator performing the historic functions of a bishop in the Methodist constituent bodies. The whole structure culminates in the General Council.

Although the unity of the whole body is signified by the name of the United Church of Christ, the membership is still classified in accordance with the three denominational categories—Congregational, Presbyterian, and Episcopal. Each denomination uniting with the others is to declare to which of the categories it chooses to adhere. This feature is not quite clear, since *all* will in reality be governed by the over-all integrated polity described above. Perhaps this feature represents a provisional stage before the contemplated organic union could become effective; or it has reference to local customs, modes of worship, and the administration of sacraments. I must confess that I am not clear on this point.

In summarizing my reactions to the proposals, I might point

out that it is obviously a far cry from the full-orbed aspirations of the maximalist ecumenicists. It quite leaves out of consideration the demands of the "Catholic" churches, thus tacitly acknowledging the insurmountable nature of the obstacles which the all-inclusive ecumenical aim presents. Unfortunately, it does not take into consideration even all "Protestant" denominations. The Episcopalians have significantly abstained from participating (Canon Wedel was present as an observer); the Lutherans and the Baptists were not represented at all. It is not difficult to understand the attitude of the Episcopalians or the Lutherans: neither their creedal nor their polity requirements were met by the Greenwich Plan. The Apostles' and the Nicene creeds were not even mentioned; nor was the historic episcopate, that *sine qua non* of the Episcopalians, included, for the Methodist bishops are not recognized as belonging to that order. The plan, accordingly, is limited to a sizable minority of Protestants in the United States (even if the bodies represented by their delegates had officially adopted the plan, which has not been done). The best that could be said for the plan is that it represents a proposal on which a limited but immediate action could be taken. But would not such a move be too hasty and might it not hinder rather than help a more adequate action later?

On the other hand, the South India Church, which was organized in 1947, after nearly thirty years of negotiations, provides more ambitious plans, particularly for the mission fields, although it likewise looks toward more distant and larger goals. Moreover, it is actually and to all intents and purposes already successfully in operation, thus scoring a considerable advantage over the Greenwich Plan. At its inception, the scheme involved four dioceses of the Anglican Province of India, the Methodist mission, and the South India Church. The usual reference to this matter in practically all treatments of it [1] omits any mention of the South India United Church and substitutes for it the Congregational and Presbyterian missions. But the United Church had been formed in 1908 from five separate

[1] Cf., for instance, J. E. Lesslie Newbigin, *The Reunion of the Church* (London, Student Christian Movement Press, Ltd., New York, Harper & Brothers, 1948). Used by permission.

missions, Congregational and Presbyterian in polity, to which a Lutheran mission was added later. This body had been at first 90 per cent Congregational, but in course of time became predominantly Presbyterianized.[2] Accordingly, both Congregationalism and Presbyterianism which had entered the Church of South India had already been modified. All parties to the new union had been thereby obliged to leave their respective communions to form a new communion. When the Lambeth Conference of 1948 was presented with the fact of the withdrawal of the four dioceses, it reluctantly accepted the *fait accompli* but expressed a hope that no similar event would happen again.[3]

The Constitution of the Church of South India follows closely the proposals of the Lambeth Quadrilateral. For its doctrinal basis, it accepts the Holy Scriptures and both the Apostles' and the Nicene creeds. The Constitution further "recognizes that episcopal, presbyteral, and congregational elements must all have their place in its [the Church's] order of life," and that "it will maintain the historic episcopate in a constitutional form"; although it explicitly affirms that such acceptance "does not commit it to any particular interpretation of episcopacy." In plain language, Apostolic succession may be held or rejected, just as the members please. As for the membership and ministry of the Church, all members of the three uniting communions were accepted at the time of union as members and ministers in full standing in the new communion. But thereafter all candidates for the ministry joining the Church and seeking ordination therein must be ordained by "the laying on of hands of the bishops and presbyters"; and bishops must be consecrated by at least three other bishops. Freedom of conviction on debatable matters is guarded by the provision that "the Church will not allow any over-riding of conscience" or impose on congregations forms of worship to which they conscientiously object.[4]

Finally it needs to be pointed out that these arrangements

[2] Bengt Sundkler, *Church of South India* (London, Lutterworth Press, 1954), p. 43. Used by permission.

[3] Albert du Bois, *The Church of South India Question* (New York, American Church Publications, 1958), p. 4.

[4] *The Constitution of the Church of South India* (Madras, The Christian Literature Society, 1956), pp. 4–12.

are only provisional. They are to last thirty years, after which period the Church itself is to determine under which conditions it would receive ministers from other churches. The Constitution states that the Church will then determine

> whether there shall continue to be any exceptions to the rule that its ministry is an episcopally ordained ministry, and generally under what conditions it will receive ministers from other Churches into its ministry. In so doing, it will give equal weight to the principle that there shall be a fully unified ministry within the Church, and to the no less fundamental principle that the Church of South India shall maintain and extend full communion and fellowship with those Churches with which the Churches from which it has been formed have severally had such fellowship. The status of those at that time already received as ministers in the Church of South India shall not be affected by any action which the Church may then take.[5]

The question uppermost in the minds of those both inside and outside the Church of South India has been: Will that communion in time become absorbed in the Anglican communion—as the non-Anglicans fear—or will it become simply another Protestant denomination—as the Anglicans fear? The first of these alternatives has been greatly strengthened by the significant sentence in the Constitution asserting: "It is the intention and expectation of the Church of South India that eventually every minister exercising a permanent ministry in it will be an episcopally ordained minister" (p. 17). Bishop Newbigin in the sermon preached on the occasion of the tenth anniversary of the founding of the Church declared that although either of these alternatives could take place, in such an eventuality the real intent of the Church would fail.

Nevertheless, it is extremely instructive to notice the treatment accorded the Church of South India by the Anglican and Protestant Episcopal communions. The Archbishop of Canterbury—a recognized ecumenical leader—prior to the union had appointed a commission to study the matter. This group published its report—known as Derby Report—in 1946. It was fairly

[5] *Ibid.*, pp. 17–18.

critical regarding doctrinal and polity "ambiguities." It was obvious that the standards by which these latter were judged were those of the Church of England and that they expected the Church of South India to conform completely to them. They particularly objected to the "communion and fellowship" with the non-episcopal churches after the expiration of the thirty-year period. The non-episcopal bodies which had entered the union in 1947 were to be so thoroughly episcopalized that they could have no hankering after "the pit from which they had been dug." Nevertheless, at the Lambeth Conference of 1948 (at which the four previously Anglican bishops of the Church of South India were *not* recognized as members), the discussion as to recognition resulted in a division of opinion, and no action was taken. It was not until in 1955 that the two convocations of Canterbury and York passed a resolution which acknowledged the bishops, presbyters, and deacons consecrated or ordained in the meantime as possessing valid orders, and extended to them some privileges in the Anglican parishes.[6]

As for the Protestant Episcopal Church, where the matter of the recognition of the Church of South India came up for discussion in October, 1958, the fight concerning it, carried on vigorously by the American Church Union—the Catholic wing of the Protestant Episcopal Church—had loomed large. Canon du Bois had insisted that the orders of the Church of South India were not valid; its doctrine of orders was deficient because it did not demand belief in apostolic succession; its faith was not orthodox, because it did not require an assent to every word of the creeds; and its sacramental doctrine was deficient. In short, to quote the good canon, "C.S.I. is a sect and a denomination in the full sense in which those terms are currently used to describe the many Protestant denominations to be found in our American communities, groups which in the past have for one reason or another departed from the One, Holy, Catholic, and Apostolic Church."[7] Fortunately, at the convention the recommendations of the Commission on Ecu-

[6] *Ibid.*

[7] Du Bois, *op. cit.*, p. 4.

menical Relations prevailed, and the Church of South India was accorded approximately the same recognition that had been granted it three years previously by the Anglicans. However, one additional limitation was added; namely, that admission to the Lord's Supper was restricted only to those who had been episcopally confirmed. Thus as one bishop remarked: "If Bishop Newbigin was invited to celebrate the communion as a true bishop in the Church of God, he would be restricted from receiving the very elements he had consecrated, even though the Prayer Book rubric commanded the celebrant to receive first of all." [8] Altogether, then, the reception afforded the Church of South India by the Anglican and Protestant Episcopal communions does not augur well for any other bodies disposed to follow that church's example.

Perhaps we have sufficiently indicated the nature of the proposals offered by these two concrete examples. I now wish to suggest what in the light of the whole discussion may be regarded as a realistic approach to the unity we seek. I do so with fear and trembling, and am far from assuming that it is anything more than another private opinion among the vast flood of similar personal views. Nevertheless, I feel an earnest desire not only to suggest a critique of such of the extant proposals as seem to ignore the obvious limitations of the ecumenical movement and therefore depart from sober reality in chasing a mirage, or are lacking in what I regard to be essentials, but to offer constructive suggestions as well.

The first and most obvious of such essentials is the recognition and acceptance of Jesus Christ as the supreme and final revelation of God. This revelation is a historical fact; hence, Christianity is a historical religion. Jesus Christ must always remain central to Christianity, and a substantial deviation from this primary requirement of faith must be regarded as inadmissible. Christianity is differentiated from other religions insofar as it is necessarily connected with the revelation of God in Jesus Christ. As Ignatius of Antioch expressed it early in the second century,

[8] Copyright 1958, Christian Century Foundation. Reprinted by permission from November 5, 1958, issue of *The Christian Century*.

"Wherever Jesus Christ is there is the Catholic Church." [9] This is, by the way, the first instance of the use of the word "Catholic." Christianity could not survive as a religious philosophy or as the Plotinian mystical "flight of the alone to the alone." Thus historical facts *do* matter. The effort to recover as precisely as possible the circumstances and the meaning of the events connected with the life of Jesus Christ and the early Church is important. The assured results of this intensive research into the historical circumstances of the first century must be retained as valid for our faith. Not that they themselves are the faith, that is, a personal commitment to God as revealed in Christ. But they are the valid presupposition of such a faith, for thus alone may God be known in His own self-revelation.

Furthermore, this implies the acceptance of the Scriptures as the witness to this revelation. This is not bibliolatry. For without a record of that revelation, how could we learn of the historical fact with which all subsequent history of Christianity is indissolubly connected? How would we know the content of that revelation as comprised in the *kerygma* of the apostolic preaching? Thus it is evident that the Church must be and remain biblical: once we leave this starting point and allow unlimited speculation or unrestrained tradition to hold sway, we are cast adrift. I am mindful of the painfully evident fact that practically all denominations profess to base themselves on the Scriptures, and yet derive from this presumably common source mutually conflicting conclusions. Nevertheless, granted this basic acknowledgment of Scriptural authority as the preeminent source of our knowledge of God, the various existing differences as to the mode of interpretation may and must be freely admitted and borne with. Only the witness of the Holy Spirit to our hearts can then be acknowledged as the authoritative means of interpretation; for He alone can lead us into an ever greater apprehension of the Truth.

In the third place, the united Church must reach an agreement on the essentials of the Christian faith. For the vast

[9] Kirsopp Lake, tr., *The Apostolic Fathers* (New York, The Macmillan Company, 1912), I, 261.

majority of Protestants, in fact of all Christians, these essentials comprise at least the dogmas of the Incarnation, of the unity and oneness of the Godhead in three self-revelations, and of the divine-human natures of our Lord in one person. The trinitarian doctrine is vitally important, in fact absolutely essential: it not only asserts in its first clause that God is one; but it goes on to affirm that this one God has revealed Himself in Jesus Christ, and abides in the hearts of His people as the Holy Spirit.

There could be no Church, that is, oneness and fellowship —*koinonia*—among its members without the Holy Spirit. This makes the Christian community essential. For that reason, an adequate concept of the Church is of tremendous significance. In this connection, I must stress once more the importance of distinguishing between the Church invisible and the Church visible. This would clarify the confusion now existing in the minds of many ecumenicists and would obviate ascribing to the former what belongs exclusively to the latter. I am amazed that some of the ecumenical leaders utterly reject the concept of the Church invisible. For instance, C. C. Morrison calls it a "fiction." For after all, unity is a spiritual concept and thus noninstitutional. Christians are indeed one if they share the mind which was in Christ Jesus, even though they differ in many doctrinal tenets and the modes of administration of the institution of the Church. Thus as a spiritual entity, as the Body of Christ, the Church is necessarily one. It is not an organization but a living organism. Accordingly, fellowship, communion of saints, a sense of oneness of believers as members of the one Body of Christ are the primary unifying means the Church possesses. These are the marks of the *koinonia*. He who breaks it by asserting superiority either of jurisdiction or of knowledge sins against love. For no individual believer possesses the whole available apprehension of truth: that belongs, at any given time and for the time being, to the totality of the members of the Church. Even then it is never complete or perfect. The revelation of God in Jesus Christ is final and complete; but the Church's apprehension of this revelation is never final or complete. Nevertheless, no one knows the truth except from within the Church. In this sense it is true that *"extra ecclesiam nulla salus,"* provided it refers to the Church invisible.

Furthermore, the Church acknowledges fellowship of believers, communion of saints, but not irresponsible submission to authority. Its order is not an enforced obedience to external authority, but free unity of believers in their common apprehension of truth and their common effort to make that truth effective in their own lives and in society. If choice must be made between unity and freedom, then let us choose freedom: for a church lacking freedom is not a true Church. God is freedom to those who love Him; He is law only to those who rebel against Him. No one can be forced to accept God's proffered grace; but once he becomes a member of Christ's body he cannot be cut off from it except by his own act.

There are many other doctrines which are no less essential—for instance, God's grace in the redemption of man from his hopeless condition. "God was in Christ, reconciling the world unto Himself." Furthermore, the Christian doctrine of man, which is particularly crucial in our days of prevailing dehumanization, must be stressed. The proclamation of the duties of the extension of God's rule in the world, and of the ultimate aims of life—these and other insights into the inexhaustible riches of God's revelation in Jesus Christ need to be formulated afresh for each age. This does not exclude the use of such ancient creeds as the Apostles', the Niceno-Constantinopolitan, and the Chalcedonian, provided they are not mandatory. Furthermore, it must be stressed much more than has been done hitherto that a reasonable liberty of interpretation, and freedom of conscientious objections, be granted. One gains the impression from reading the literature of the movement that some ecumenicists are altogether too ready to surrender the hard-won freedoms of the Reformation and those gained at a great cost since.

Thus the Church is freedom limited by love, for religion without freedom is a contradiction in terms. It is a brotherhood, a fellowship. The only bond of fellowship within the Church is love, and love cannot be forced or externally imposed. As Father Florovsky has written: "The Church accepts into her bosom only the free."[10] And Apostle Paul similarly exhorts the Galatians, "For freedom Christ has set us free." To which Luther adds his earnest plea in the famous treatise on *The Freedom of Christian Man* when he writes: "A Christian man is a perfectly free lord of all and subject to none. A Christian man is a perfectly dutiful servant of all, subject to everyone." Thus the most effective way in which the ecumenical quest may be furthered is to proceed by way of *"maximal community and minimal doctrinal consensus."*[11] But this is not to reject every doctrinal consensus prior to union on the ground that Christianity is primarily a way of life.[12] After all, life must be guided by principles.

But since no one can distinguish with certainty and accuracy who are the members of the Church invisible—the names of the saints are written only in the Book of Life, not on the church rolls—it is extraordinarily difficult to organize congregations composed only of saints. The Anabaptists tried it. Our Congregational forefathers followed the same concept early in the seventeenth century when they attempted to build the Kingdom of God on the rocky shores of New England, but within a generation they found it necessary to modify the plan by adopting the "Half Way Covenant." I do not know what fraction of the covenant is left nowadays. Many other earnest Protestant groups from time to time have attempted to limit church membership "to saints only," but with the same sad results.

We therefore conclude that the historic pattern of church membership, consisting of undifferentiated stands of wheat mixed with tares, of saints and sinners, or rather of sinners on the way to sainthood and those who are just plain garden-variety sinners, is the normal and inevitable one. The Church may be likened to a piece of iron in the fire, permeated to greater or less degree by the heat. The heat is dependent upon the iron as

[10] Georges Florovsky, *Puti russkago bogosloviya* (Paris, YMCA Press, 1937), p. 276.

[11] Outler, *The Christian Tradition . . .* , p. 96.

[12] C. C. Morrison, "Light on the Pathway to Unity," *The Christian Century*, 46 (1929), 8.

much as the iron is on the heat. Some Christians or churches are barely lukewarm, others radiate white heat. Most occupy perhaps the middle ground. Applying this analogy to our discussion of the relation of the invisible and visible Church, we now conclude that any absolute separation between them is not possible, and hence that when we ascribe unity in Christ to the Church invisible, this unity is shared by the Church visible to the degree to which that body is dominated by the mind of Christ. It is in this sense that the federalists and ecumenicists alike are right in striving for the outward unity of the Church. Where some of them are not always clear in their conception of the task is when they do not seem to realize that this latter kind of unity must necessarily be relative, because the mind of Christ is not fully dominant in the Church visible. Consequently, the unity movement must have for its first objective making the mind of Christ regnant within all Christians that Christ may truly become the Lord of all. Unity is not attainable by organizational means and schemes alone.

I am aware that many other important doctrinal considerations could be mentioned if one aimed at comprehensiveness, which I do not; moreover, I also have in mind the staggering number of various interpretations, additions, emphases, and other variations which would properly come into consideration in connection with the basic Christian message. But I cheerfully yield to all and sundry a reasonable liberty of interpretation, provided the essentials are not thereby subverted. The Gospel message is necessarily subject to varying apprehension—we shall never completely apprehend the fullness of the revelation of God in Jesus Christ, for "now we see through a glass, darkly"—and likewise our understanding of them is subject to varying conceptual and verbal expressions in conformity with the time in which we live. But this must never be an excuse for "throwing out the baby with the bath." These are then the principles which must govern the formulation of the Church's faith. I doubt that the Apostles' and the Nicene creeds are adequate to accomplish what I have suggested; but as partial statements, and assuming reasonable liberty of interpretation of some of their articles, or as the ancient blessed phrase had it "for the substance of doctrine," they are acceptable as at least partially fulfilling the requirements.

But we must furthermore consider the organization of the Church. As has been stated before, this is *not* an item necessary to salvation, but on the other hand it is not altogether unimportant. The same principle of unity in freedom limited by love applies to the recognition of a valid ministry for the entire body, irrespective of the mode of ordination. Both episcopal and non-episcopal ordination must be unequivocally recognized as equally valid. This recognition must then logically involve intercommunion. The two sacraments—baptism and the Lord's Supper—would then without difficulty be recognized as "the seals of the divine promise" and as "outward symbols of an inner grace." But their significance or mode of administration is to be left to the various traditions that would still exist within the united Church. Thus the historic polities—Congregational, Presbyterian, and Episcopal (not requiring the apostolic succession for the latter's validity)—are in their different ways good, or are good for different ends. They must be recognized as permanently valuable and as such should continue to exist side by side. For they cannot be integrated—homogenized, so to speak—in such a way that they would either retain or enhance their separate essential qualities. For that reason I do not see any overwhelming reason for surrendering them; in fact, any attempt to do so would neutralize the distinctive feature of each, or more likely result in superimposing one—the Episcopal, most probably—upon the others. Moreover, the attempt would really mean that we regard a particular polity as essential, while it should be treated as non-essential. In this as in all other aspects let freedom within the bonds of love be our guide. The aim I would stress could thus be termed "diversity-in-unity," not uniformity. Accordingly, the pattern of unified Church which I wish to further would be analogous to the organization of the government of the United States, with the central federal government possessing delegated powers over matters of common concern, while the constituent bodies retain their individual denominational usages and polities. Or if you like Bishop Dun's figure of speech better, we may picture it as an architectural construct comprising a central building with outlying structures connected with it. But I have a sneaking suspicion that the central organization, no matter how carefully delimited as to its powers, would still possess such overweening authority as to be detrimental to the freedoms of the constituent bodies. The temptation of any such centralized body toward bureaucracy is so great as to be to all intents and purposes unavoidable. The example of the functioning of almost any denominational "high brass" is all too common proof of it.

I should like to suggest, in addition to the two figures of speech given above, one that I like better because it avoids the implication of the mechanical or legalistic features of the over-all central organizations. I should like to compare the central organ of the united Church to an orchestra, where it is essential that the various instruments take part and each kind play its own assigned role, and yet all together produce a harmony, under the leadership of the conductor, which could not be achieved otherwise. A bass drum cannot take the place of a piccolo, and a tuba could never be mistaken for a violin. The diversity of instruments is not a scandal of disunion, but a necessary contributory element in producing the orchestral harmony. If fault there should be, it would not be in the diversity, but in noncooperation of one instrument with another and in disregarding the leadership of the conductor. It is on this pattern I should like to see the Church organized.

By this time it must be abundantly clear that for myself I do not envisage the coming Church as ecumenical in the true and maximal sense of the word. I have no hope that for the immediate or even foreseeable future such plans as I have suggested would prove acceptable to the great Roman Catholic or Eastern Orthodox communions. Perhaps, it would not prove immediately acceptable to all Protestant communions, either. It is for that reason that I would urge a realistic approach characterized by a certain modesty of aim. Reaching for the moon may easily result in losing both the moon and what could otherwise be within our grasp—unless somebody could invent an ecclesiastical sputnik which would reach the moon! The only true failure would consist in not securing the more modest results I suggested, and in the dissipation of the enthusiasm and consecrated energies which the movement has generated. I plead for striving for these attainable goals, while we hope for greater things to come.

Since what I am proposing is not "ecumenicity," am I advocating Pan-Protestantism? I would not insist even on that goal as the absolute and irreducible minimum. The way to start is to start. One of the earliest Congregational worthies (who alas! did not remain a Congregational worthy) was Robert Browne, who wrote a treatise on *A Reformation without tarrying for Anie.* For many years I had been puzzling who Anie could be, until at last I understood that Browne insisted that no reformation can be accomplished if one waits until everybody climbs on the bandwagon. Let the reformation begin with those who are really ready and willing to accept the essence of the objectives sought. But I also recognize the contrary danger of too precipitous action, which might make a larger result more difficult to attain. Nevertheless, the alternative of the all-or-nothing policy might very well be nothing.

What then can we reasonably expect of this realistic approach? First of all, the unification of the existing communions of the same ecclesiastical family. *The Year Book of American Churches for 1959* lists 267 religious bodies. This is often held up to ridicule or condemnation. But the vast majority of the Protestant communions are comprised in eight denominational families—Adventist, Baptist, Disciples, Congregationalist, Lutheran, Mennonite, Methodist, and Presbyterian; and in two Catholic communions, the Roman Catholic and Eastern Orthodox. The Protestant Episcopal Church chooses to divide its loyalties between the Protestants and Catholics. Of the rest, thirty-five have a thousand or less members each, seven having fewer than one hundred members and one of them as few as twenty. Yet they are cited as "denominations"! If the various subdivisions of the eight above-named Protestant communions were to coalesce, and the Catholic bodies were to do likewise—for they also are divided, the Eastern Orthodox having nineteen bodies, one of them consisting of one congregation with thirty-nine members—the vast majority of Christians in the United States would be organized in eleven communions. If the alternate plan, of organizing the Protestant denominations according to their polity, were adopted, their number would be reduced to three! To be sure, this would not rid us of smaller denominations and splinter groups. But no conceivable plan would: for where there is liberty, there are bound to be differences.

On the world scale, support should be extended to the World Council of Churches insofar as it strives to federate the separated Christian communions. But for the present I would join those members of the Council who adhere to and advocate its present federative structure, although I hope it may be gradually made more effective. In other words, my sympathies lie with the group I have called federalist, rather than with the ecumenicists. These remarks are to be understood in the spirit of the principles I have discussed above.

In conclusion, let me reiterate that I regard the quest for unity as one of the most significant and potentially the most beneficial of modern movements within the Church. Its ultimate failure would not consist so much in nonattainment of the highest objectives of unification of the entire Christendom, as in neglecting to gain what can reasonably be expected at present—the elimination of the non-essential, often fortuitous divisions of the existing denominations. Some separations had been the result of causes no longer existing. Many of the doctrinal causes of separation are non-essential, and could be removed with greater or less difficulty, being capable of interpretations acceptable to the contending parties. It is in these aspects where the healing ministry of the movement could be applied with the greatest chance of success. But above all, we must remember that real unity is a spiritual entity, not an external organization. It is the cultivation of this irenic spirit of mutual understanding and fellowship—the *koinonia*—without which all other efforts would be in vain. It is in the possession of the mind of Christ that we form the Body of Christ, in which we are truly one!